Coaching
CHARACTER
at Home

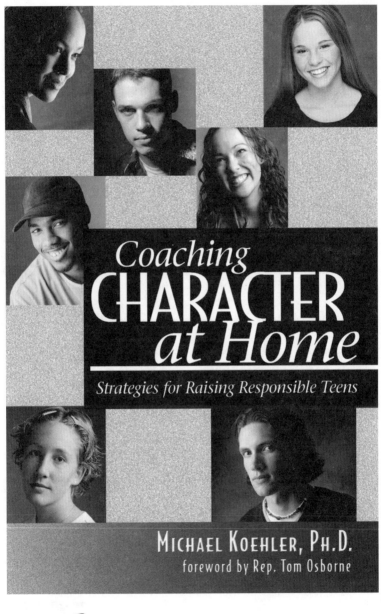

Coaching
CHARACTER
at Home

Strategies for Raising Responsible Teens

MICHAEL KOEHLER, PH.D.
foreword by Rep. Tom Osborne

SORIN BOOKS   Notre Dame, Indiana

www.sorinbooks.com

International Standard Book Number: 1-893732-48-7

Cover and text design by Brian C. Conley

Printed and bound in the United States of America.

Library of Congress Cataloging-in-Publication Data
Koehler, Mike, 1938-
  Coaching character at home : strategies for raising responsible teens / Michael Koehler.
    p. cm.
  ISBN 1-893732-48-7 (pbk.)
  1. Parent and teenager. 2. Parenting. 3. Character. 4. Responsibility in adolescence. 5. Maturation (Psychology) I. Title.
HQ799.15 .K64 2003
649'.125--dc21
                                        2002013326
                                          CIP

For any character I possess, I want to thank Sister Mary St. Elyce, who in eighth grade shared a warm embrace and the business end of her ruler in equal measure. Thanks to Coach George Kelly, who at Marquette and Nebraska taught me that caring relationships go well beyond the football field. Thanks to my father-in-law, Bud Sexmith, who taught by example the values of self-control and family love. To my grandchildren: Eric Michael, Cassie Jean, and Michael David, and to former athletes like Jeff Johnson, Bobby Dziedziech, Brian Barbour, Charlie Talbot, and hundreds of others, thanks for showing each day that character is important to young people, too.

And to my wife, Pat, thanks for continuing to teach me the spiritual and emotional power of unconditional love.

Acknowledgments

This book never would have happened were it not for my agent, Jane Jordan Browne, who is blissfully relentless in her attempts to get me into the trade market. She received help from her partner, Scott Mendel, who continues to nudge and push in his own inimitable way. The manuscript would never have developed without the remarkable editorial insight of Janie McAdams and Bob Hamma. Both were invaluable. Also invaluable was my wife, Pat, who honored our marriage in spite of my incessant requests to "read this for me and tell me how it sounds!"

The author must also acknowledge coaches like George Kelly, Tom Osborne, and Frank Lenti, who continue to make their mark on the minds and hearts of kids everywhere and who shared a sense of direction with me.

Contents

Foreword

Character is critical to the future of our nation and world. The character of our young people will come to define the character of our country as a whole. For over thirty-six years as a father, coach, educator, and mentor, I have witnessed an unraveling of the culture in America. Our values have changed, and not for the better. Juvenile crime, drug use, pregnancy, violence, and absenteeism from school have skyrocketed in recent years. We can—and must—work to correct this trend. I believe that athletics provide a medium through which young people can develop character.

Too often the needs of our young people and the time and attention necessary to develop and cultivate strong character are neglected. However, our young people are directly influenced by the people around them—for better or for worse. I have learned as a parent, coach, and educator how strong an influence you can have on young people. I encourage coaches and educators to embrace this ability and work to cultivate positive growth in our kids.

Coaches are not parents. However, they can reinforce positive lessons taught at home. A young man may spend as much time or more with his coach than with his parents. Parents and coaches can help their players develop character by:

- Acknowledging and demonstrating that character is more than what we do or what we have to do. Character is who we are. Parents should serve as role models of not only doing the right thing, but doing the right thing because they want to.
- Emphasizing the similarity in the relationships between practice and game-time performance and parental relationships and lifetime decisions.
- Motivating young people and helping young people build self-motivation.

- Promoting positivism. Athletes often credit their successful performances to self-confidence, focus on performance, positive self-talk, and an emphasis on performance rather than the outcome of the game or contest. Parents and coaches alike can instill the understanding that effort means more than outcome.
- Believing in the young people they coach.

Coaches and parents must live what they teach. Mike Koehler, my friend and the author of this book, has lived the lessons found here. Sports and the lessons he learned therein taught him the self-discipline he previously lacked. Despite suffering a cerebral hemorrhage that ended his playing career at the University of Nebraska, Mike has dedicated himself to bringing character to the national spotlight, where it belongs, and to bettering the lives of young people in America. I am pleased that he has published this work. It redefines character beyond your possessions and your outward actions to your individual essence.

Rep. Tom Osborne

Introduction

Character education, an intriguing new idea buried in the middle of the newspaper a few years ago, is grabbing headlines today. It's a hot topic for educators and politicians alike and many schools are already running with it. Character education, at least in concept, is growing nationwide. Teachers are seeking and creating all kinds of ideas and formulating curricula to develop more character in their students.

The concept is even more appealing to parents. Many of them are confused and frightened by the violence in our nation's schools, the growing selfishness of kids everywhere, and the rebellion and inconsideration in their own children. I share their concerns and, as a football coach for thirty-one years, have experienced the not-so-gradual changes in the behavior of kids and young adults. Within the past several decades, swearing, cheating, finger-flipping, tailgating, and even drive-by shootings have become disturbingly common-place, even in our smallest and most isolated communities.

Self-control and mutual respect are giving way to self-indulgence and mutual antagonism. Senseless violence is esca-lating because some of us are unable to control our anger. Prominent athletes are teaching our kids that it's good to be bad. High ranking politicians are proving that absolute power corrupts absolutely. And talk shows and soap operas are redefining our notions of what is normal in our society.

Parents are asking themselves and each other, "What is happening to our kids?" They have become confused about their responsibilities to their own children. Many have become hesitant to act firmly and confidently, and at times are afraid to risk the anger of children who have learned defiance from prominent media personalities.

Chest-bumping, trash talking, and gratuitous violence have transformed media and sports role models into role muddles. Adolescence is tough enough on kids. But when they are denied consistent help from significant adults in their lives, they fail to understand and survive the developmental milestones that confuse and anger them and that contain the potential for future tragedy.

As a coach, I was able to provide such help. I was fortunate to share a love of the game with my kids and to use that bond to promote self-control and mutual respect. I was never confused about my responsibilities to my athletes. Normalcy was nothing more than hard work, teamwork, and the joy of competition. I didn't permit chest-bumping and trash talk, and I demanded the character and the courage that Hemingway defined as "grace under pressure." I expected a certain elegance in each of my kids, because I knew that it was a visible expression of character.

What is character? Character is the quality of knowing and wanting to do the right thing, then actually doing it. As such, character involves not only an understanding of integrity, morality, and spirituality but a willingness to reflect that understanding in our personal behavior. Children must *know*, then *do* what is right. And they need our help. I believe my experiences as a coach can help you as a parent be more effective in building character in your adolescent children.

Most teachers already know that character development is nothing new to coaches. Self-disciplined attitudes and behavior have been demanded on practice fields and in gymnasiums for as long as coaches have carried clipboards and whistles. Coaches are so influential with their athletes that teachers frequently call on them for help with certain kids. For that reason, coaching principles and strategies are forming the foundation for character education programs in many schools.

The principles at work in these programs can work in the home, too. Helping a child develop his or her full potential does not depend on what material benefits parents provide. It doesn't even depend on what the adolescent succeeds in accomplishing, but rather on the self-discipline and the moral substance he or she develops. Good parents, like good coaches, must understand that "success" transcends what their children do or have; it's a function of who and what they *are*. And who they are depends on a consistency of behavior that comes from self-discipline.

Such consistency is the key to character, and character is at the core of every winner. Coaches want their athletes to understand that character is getting up when they think they can't. It's consistently pushing beyond their limits, doing something they don't believe they can do—or don't want to do. It's looking at adversity as opportunity, possible failure as challenge, competition as a consistent refusal to lose.

Parents, like coaches, must be constantly alert to opportunities that reinforce such positive behaviors. Coaches drill fundamental skills into their athletes. Similarly, parents must drill positive behaviors into their children. Doing chores around the house, volunteering for community activities, speaking respectfully to friends and acquaintances, using appropriate language, and reflecting good upbringing are the "fundamentals" that parents drill into their children.

With such repetitive training, character becomes almost intuitive. It is formed unconsciously, like a good habit. A well-trained athlete might spontaneously find himself "in the zone," sinking a succession of three-pointers or grooving a fast ball unconsciously. Ask the gymnast how she nailed that perfect ten, and she'll tell you she doesn't know; it just felt right. So it is with character.

Athletes with character are winners. They commit to their coaches and teammates. They develop the self-control that curbs impulsive and misguided behavior. Their desire to do the right thing becomes a functioning and integral part of who they are. They are dependable, and, as a result, they are happy. Their character spurs them on during good times and sustains them during bad times.

There's an old saying in sport: "Winners win; losers lose." It's amazingly accurate, not just for athletes but for people in all walks of life. Some people always win; they win at everything they do. Others, no matter what they do, keep losing. They walk around like so many cartoon characters with rain clouds over their heads, spouting grandiose expectations, but stumbling over one flop after another.

How do we help our children to be winners? Encouraging their belief in themselves is certainly a good place to start. And belief in oneself depends on a philosophical framework that guides their behavior. During my thirty-some years of coaching football, our coaching staff developed a philosophy that evolved during our first ten years together. It was a philosophy that guided our behavior as coaches and eventually made winners of our athletes.

We called these principles the "7 Cs." They involve seven essential behaviors our players had to exhibit if they hoped to prove to us that they had the strength of character to make a contribution to our program. It seems to me that they also represent what parents want for and from their children, especially as they navigate the adolescent years.

The Seven Cs

- Connectedness: shared enthusiasm for a common interest
- Control: self-control, self-reflection, self-evaluation, and self-correction
- Commitment: personal investment, complete and focused involvement
- Consistency: firmness of purpose, the refusal to quit
- Cooperation: the willingness to work with others, to share success and failure
- Conscience: empathy for others, understanding the difference between right and wrong
- Competition: the willingness to make the effort to win and to realize that this effort is more important than the outcome

Each of these seven principles was pounded into me and my fellow coaches when we played football. I was the starting fullback and outside linebacker at Marquette University and, when they dropped football, transferred to the University of Nebraska. I was fortunate to play for Lisle Blackburn, Bob Devaney, George Kelly, and, for a short time, Tom Osborne, four coaches with uncompromised principles who modeled and expected strong character both on and off the field. Their impact on me as an athlete and as a man has echoed through my children and thousands of my own athletes who keep these principles alive in their own behavior and in the way they now raise their children.

The principles are tried and true standards of effective child rearing. What made them special for our players was the immediate relevance they had during competition and, we hoped, after the football season. Over the years, the kids created mottoes such as "Nail the 7 Cs" and "Hail the 7 Cs." We decided they could do whatever they wanted as long as they didn't "fail the 7 Cs." That was unacceptable—and they knew it. So our challenge as coaches was to "sell the 7 Cs," to make sure our own behavior was consistent with each principle, recognizing that young people need models much more than they need critics.

These seven principles form the framework of the book. Each "C" is a chapter. Each is supported by a wealth of subheadings that illustrate effective child-rearing principles, enlightening and entertaining pointers that provide a sense of direction for parents. Each is also illustrated and supported by media stories and anecdotes from my personal experiences as a coach and a parent as well as the experiences of friends and colleagues. In addition, many of the subheadings within each chapter contain dialogues that illustrate suggested ways to influence character development in kids.

Years ago, I was complaining to a friend's father that I couldn't find a starting quarterback. He asked me how many kids were trying out for the position. I said about five or six. I'll never forget his response: "That's what you're getting paid for, kid—coach 'em!" With just two words, he told me to stop whining and do my job. For years afterward, "Coach 'em" became my answer for filling key positions. Whenever a player couldn't do the job, I asked myself, "What's the problem? He can't learn—or I can't coach?" Each day offered the chance for me to be a better teacher.

"Coach 'em" also became the answer for developing character in virtually all of my players. Whenever a kid got out of line, I asked myself variations of the same question: "How much of this problem is my fault?" Character is something kids learn, so I challenged myself to teach character as well as fundamental skills and strategy. Most parents don't carry whistles and clipboards, but "Coach 'em" can be as important for you as it was for me.

1

CONNECTEDNESS
Sharing Common Interests and Much More

It was one of my first pep talks. It certainly wasn't my best, but it was one of my most memorable. What I remember most was not my desire to win the game or to stir the kids into a frenzy, but my sudden awareness that every eye in the locker room was on me. Every fist and jaw was clenching and unclenching as I spoke. Every chest was pumping air faster and faster. I didn't think my speech was that good, but those kids simply wanted to connect with me! They were filled with a need to play well in the second half of the game, and they wanted me to say something, anything that would create a fire in their bellies.

That awareness helped me realize the intimacy of the relationship between players and coaches. You see, I was well aware that I wasn't, and had never been, an inspirational genius. I knew halfway through the speech that I was only a partner in the growing intensity we all felt. Biologists call it a symbiotic relationship. Football coaches call it love of the game. Parents call it family ties. Whatever it was that day many years ago, it resulted in a connectedness that everyone in the locker room shared. Without that connectedness, no amount of shouting or cajoling on my part would have worked any motivational magic.

That day was the first in a long line of learning experiences for me. As my coaching career unfolded and my formal education increased, I learned that kids have a variety of emotional and relational needs that must be satisfied, but I was surprised to learn that they also need to accept blame and to admire and yield to a superior. My job as a coach, and later as a parent, was to help satisfy those needs, especially the ones dealing with accepting blame and yielding to a superior!

Basically, I learned that children are self-directed, so I didn't waste a lot of time "motivating" them. Instead, I *helped* them satisfy their own motivational needs. As time went on, I depended less on pre-game and halftime speeches and more on my ability to recognize their effort, to create a sense of family, to provide feedback, to promote their self-assessment, as well as to encourage their admiration and support for me as their coach.

Until we as parents acknowledge the basic needs that truly motivate kids, such as their needs to belong, to achieve, and to be recognized, we are kidding ourselves into thinking that we direct our kids' lives. As I helped to satisfy the needs of my athletes and to understand the connectedness that held us together, I realized that the same could happen with my three daughters. Coaching helped me to become a better parent. Let me share some of what I learned.

What Is Connectedness?

Connectedness means much more than simply sharing interests. It involves going through life together, like a team, sharing joys, feelings, uncertainties, concerns, ideas, and experiences. Connectedness accepts the notion that love is life's most powerful spiritual force.

HOW COACHES ACHIEVE CONNECTEDNESS:

For the Love of the Game

Coaches connect by sharing a love of the game and mutual respect with their players. They share hard work, anxiety about the contest, and the ability to handle defeat with dignity, winning with humility. They sweat together, fret together, commiserate and celebrate together. They join hands against adversity and high five after a victory. When the contest is on the line, coaches exhort players to commit with their heads, their hearts, and their bodies to a total team effort.

Watch How I Do It

Good coaches care about kids, usually unconditionally. Their only qualifiers are that players work hard, commit to their teammates and coaches, and refuse to quit. As football coaching great Vince Lombardi once said, "Winning isn't everything. The *will* to win is everything." All good coaches agree with Lombardi. Making the effort to win is far more important than the outcome of any contest. When our kids commit heart and soul to any effort, they are winners, no matter what the outcome. Good coaches reflect such a commitment in their own behavior.

HOW PARENTS ACHIEVE CONNECTEDNESS:

We're All in This Together

Families share common bonds and mutual love. Parents love unconditionally. While you have to place limits on certain aspects of your adolescents' lives, your love must be unbound. When parents find the time to sweat, fret, commiserate, and celebrate together with their children, they connect with them.

Such connectedness involves communication, the willingness to sit down and talk—really talk—about the child's problems, apprehensions, happy moments, or future plans.

During these times, moms and dads must be parents to their children, not buddies. I never met the fifteen-year-old who wanted a forty-year-old buddy. Being a buddy may seem easier during moments of stress, but it rarely provides the objective and sometimes firm direction kids require. Connectedness binds; it doesn't blind.

"Do as I Do"

Our children must learn to form relationships, interact, collaborate on problems, forgive, help each other, accept blame, and admire others from us. They do as we do. When we involve kids in family decision making, admire them, forgive them, interact with them, recognize specific accomplishments, and practice accepting blame and even apologize when our own behavior is not what it should be, we are modeling connectedness for them.

I apologized more than once after games when my play-calling fell short and we lost the game. Coaches and parents make mistakes too. When we do, we discover a remarkable opportunity to model the adult way to accept the consequences of our actions. When we stand tall and accept blame, kids are more inclined to do it too.

Connectedness Is Revealing

Connectedness helps our teens and pre-teens to understand the importance of their contributions, to be accountable for outcomes, and to know whether or not those outcomes are satisfactory. The tragedy at the World Trade Center not only underscored the importance of the contributions of police and firemen, but of volunteers, and of the several heroes who were thrust suddenly into life's ultimate challenge. And they all delivered. Their connectedness has become our connectedness. We are all much closer because of their dedication and valor.

We Each Do Our Share

Although participation in athletics involves a less dramatic commitment, it does enable kids to use their talents and skills to full advantage and to dedicate themselves to causes larger than themselves. Coaches encourage kids to see how their contributions fit into the whole picture. They help them to see how their involvement affects the lives of their teammates and coaches and to make decisions regarding strategy and performance. Coaches give immediate and clear feedback regarding the effects of each athlete's performance.

We achieve connectedness as parents when we encourage our children to use their talents and skills to help the family and themselves. Our challenge is to help them understand the individual roles of family members and the importance of their own role and the ways these roles affect everyone else in the family. Give kids periodic feedback regarding their behavior: "We get concerned, Tom, when you behave that way in class; people begin to wonder what kind of family you're from." Or: "Tom, I noticed how you helped Tammy with her homework last night. I think she realized that sometimes it's not so bad to have a big brother!" I know that kids wear out parents faster than their shoes, but, tired or not, it doesn't take a lot of time to recognize the good our kids do.

Don't Just Praise—Recognize

Coaches who know how to teach realize that such feedback doesn't simply involve praise; it focuses on specific recognition: "Great job catching the ball at its highest point," "Good base on your block; it helped your balance." Many good coaches understand on the other hand that general praise ("Nice job" or "Way to go") fosters continued dependency; kids depend on their coaches for more of the same. Effective coaches know that only specific recognition provides the details that not only improve performance but encourage independence.

As parents, I suggest we use praise sparingly. Specific recognition provides the kind of connectedness that fosters independence. It provides guidelines for future behavior. General praise, such as "Nice job last night," promotes dependence on the parent for more praise and a kind of connectedness that doesn't help the child.

* * * * * * *

Because a knowledge of results is so important to kids, learn and use the dialoguing technique called "Recognizing." It illustrates the difference between general praise and specific recognition.

Dialogue - Recognizing

Coach to Player

Coach: Yes! That's exactly what I'm looking for!

Player: Yeah, not bad if I say so myself!

Coach: Not bad? It was great! You got off the ground, extended your arms, and caught the ball at its highest point! (Feedback as well as specific recognition of the athlete's performance) You screened off the defender with your body. He didn't have a chance. (More specific recognition)

Player: Yeah, I guess that drill paid off.

Parent to Child

Parent: Your English teacher cornered me in the store today.

Child: Did he tell you about my attempted overthrow of the principal?

Parent: No, wise guy, he told me about your term paper. He said it was one of the best ones he's seen all year.

Child: Did a promised A put a smile on your face?

Parent: Frankly, yes, but I watched you write that paper, and the grade is only a small part of what you accomplished.

Child: Come on, what's better than an A?

Parent: Organization, research, hard work, common sense. (Feedback) I saw you get right to work as soon as you got home the last several days. (Specific recognition) You spent hours just on the computer! And the actual composition had to be a whole lot tougher. (More specifics)

Child: Hey, you really know what goes into this stuff. Maybe you can do my next one!

Parent: OK! And you can do the dinners for the rest of the year.

Connected Kids Make a Difference

Connecting with kids helps them feel that they make a difference. Kids are, by nature, self-centered. The developmental milestones they must negotiate en route to adulthood provoke a self-focus that is so intense that many kids are unable to see beyond the tips of their noses. In addition, today's growing emphasis on money and "things" has led to a selfishness that further disconnects them from family and friends.

HOW COACHES ACHIEVE CONNECTEDNESS:

Everyone's Job Is Important

Sports connects kids to each other and helps them realize the value of their contributions. The first-stringer contributes during the contest; the second-stringer contributes during practice. Both contributions help the team. Good coaches understand this and routinely remind their players of the contributions each makes to the success of the team.

Feeling Needed

A coach I knew went so far as to tell his players to select the captains before each game, one of whom had to be the third- or fourth-stringer who practiced hardest that week. It was an honor to the player who was selected, but, more important, it reminded everyone on the team of the daily contributions they all make. They all felt needed.

HOW PARENTS ACHIEVE CONNECTEDNESS:

Kids Need Models More Than They Need Critics

Make your children feel needed. The easiest way to help kids make a difference is to ask yourself, "How do *I* make a difference?" Do I volunteer in the community? Do I routinely reach out to elderly neighbors or to those touched by tragedy? Am I spontaneously friendly with friends and acquaintances, even with strangers?

If answers to these and similar questions are YES, invite your kids to connect with you when you are acting for the good of others. Kids need models, inspirational models.

Fortunately, such models are sitting at the dinner table with them just about every night. Television, movies, sports pages, and literature provide some role models but generally do more to sensationalize role *muddles,* social anomalies that undermine parental values. The most important role models in any child's life are his or her parents.

We Love You and We Need You

Help your kids capitalize on their interests and strengths. If your teen likes to cook, have him cook the entire meal once a week. If your daughter is curious about science, ask her to investigate the problem of all those oak leaves killing the grass every fall. If the house needs to be painted, have the kids determine when and how they can help. If Tom's grandparents are visiting this weekend, expect him to be home to spend some time with them. Sometimes we need Tom's help; sometimes we just need Tom.

Connectedness "Makes It Happen!"

Kids who feel needed, who know that they make a difference, connect with their worlds in positive ways. Educator Tom Sergiovanni notes,

> When [children] experience meaningfulness, control, and personal responsibility, they are functioning more as "origins" than "pawns." An origin believes that behavior is determined by his or her own choosing. A pawn, by contrast, believes that behavior is determined by external forces beyond his or her control.

Coaches and parents want children to be "origins," responsible for their own behavior, eager to make a difference. When adolescents feel like pawns, they become disconnected—frustrated, even alienated. When this happens, their grades suffer, relationships at home and in school suffer, and countless others suffer when violence becomes their response to such frustration.

When kids are encouraged to make decisions about the choices available to them, they feel a sense of control. They are connected. Too many choices, particularly conflicting choices, can overwhelm kids, so we want to help them maintain perspective. But the opportunity to choose gives them a sense of power and identifies the parent as a helpmate rather than a boss.

You're in Control

Gyms and practice fields resonate with demands to "make it happen!" Coaches expect their athletes to take control of every contest, to make a difference for their teams: "If there's no lane to the basket, get there anyway!" "Nail that dismount! Make it happen!" Then, if athletes get the chance to dialogue about the right dismount or the best move to the basket, they feel a sense of control.

When "make it happen" is repeated often enough, kids not only connect with their coaches, but they discover that they can control events and produce outcomes. And when they get the additional chance to choose, they make a commitment that keeps them on target. They even start believing that they can make things happen elsewhere in their lives. When the young gymnast pushes beyond her fears and flip-flops for the first time on the balance beam, she also learns to overcome her fears on her first job or when she experiences adversity in her life.

Learn to Disconnect

To teach your kids how to make things happen, connect—and disconnect—with them at strategic times. Connecting means being warm, accepting, and attentive. Psychologists tell us that the easiest way to establish rapport is to simply nod or to paraphrase what kids say. They remind us that it isn't necessary to have all the answers or to control the conversation. In fact, such control can destroy rapport. Connecting means caring, sharing control, and being respectful.

This may sound contradictory, but there are times when parents must strategically *dis*connect. Youngsters fail to learn how to make things happen when parents do everything for them. Find opportunities to get kids to choose, to make decisions about their lives. Disconnecting once in a while actually empowers them.

Such disconnecting puts the "self" in self-control. In that regard, one of the most important things a parent can say to a child is, "That's too bad, honey, *what do you plan to do about it?*" When Cindy calls you at work to tell you she forgot her basketball uniform, don't volunteer to drive home to get it. Ask her what she plans to do about it.

When Tom tells you that he doesn't know the meaning of "synergy," say to him, "Yes, not knowing the meaning of a word can really throw you sometimes. What do you plan to do about it?" When Cindy says, "Wow, this blouse is really wrinkled!" respond by saying, "It sure is! I don't think you're going to want to wear it in that condition." Then smile and ask, "What do you plan to do about it?" Pretty soon Tom will stop asking you for definitions and reach for the dictionary, and Cindy will discover how to use an ironing board.

Kids learn by doing. Telling them how to be self-reliant is like telling them how to be confident. Self-reliance and confidence are qualities kids learn by handling the mechanics of their lives. The more *we* get them off the hook, the more often they get hung up. Kids have to take control of their lives, especially

when they don't want to. Connecting and strategically disconnecting with kids to promote their self-reliance encourages self-
confidence and cultivates positive self-concepts.

* * * * * * *

As a dialoguing technique, "choosing" can be very helpful.
It gives the child a sense of ownership. Notice that "choosing"
gives kids the chance to decide about not only the "What" but
the "How" and "When."

Dialogue - Choosing

COACH TO PLAYER

Coach: It's not going to be easy blocking that tackle, especially when he lines up in the gap. (Identify the need) What do you guys want to do when we run the inside belly? (Open the door to choices)

First player: We can cross block him. (First chance to choose) He's giving us a good angle.

Coach: Yeah, what else?

Second player: I could reach block him to seal him. (Second chance to choose)

First player: What if we wheel block it? That'll give us an angle on him from the outside, and the guard can kick out the defensive end. (Third chance to choose)

Coach: Yeah, good ideas. Which do you want to do?

Second player: I think Tom had a good idea. Let's wheel block it. If that guy lines up in the gap, I'll signal it with a "W" word. (Final choice results in commitment)

Coach: OK, let's do it. Make it happen, boys! (Commitment is acknowledged)

PARENT TO CHILD

Parent: Tom, do me a favor. Come on outside with me for a minute.

Child: Sure, what's up?

Parent: The house needs painting, and I need some help making a couple decisions. (Identify the need)

Child: I'm great with decisions, but I don't have a lot of time for painting.

Parent: Look how this side is flaking. (Disregard Tom's excuse) What color do you think we ought to paint it?

Child: I'm used to its color now; I like it. (First chance to choose)

Parent:	You know, so do I. Maybe that's what we should do. And I am going to need your help. (Open the door to choices)
Child:	Come on, Dad, I don't know when I can find the time.
Parent:	Yeah, I know you're busy. So am I, but this thing has to get done. How can we do this and get everything else done? (Second chance to choose)
Child:	Well, maybe I can get a couple of the guys to come over and help, but we can't do it for a couple weeks.
Parent:	Sounds great! Name the date.
Child:	Let me talk to the guys, but I guess we can shoot for two weeks from Saturday. (Final choice results in commitment)
Parent:	I'll put it on the calendar! (Commitment is acknowledged)

Dialogue - Pushing

The technique called "pushing" is also very helpful. Sometimes, kids have to be "pushed" in the right direction—nicely:

COACH TO PLAYER

Player:	Hey, Coach, this field is a mess! I haven't been able to field one ground ball!
Coach:	Why? What's happening?
Player:	The infield looks like it hasn't been raked in a year.
Coach:	Well, what are you going to do about it? (Push player to make decision)
Player:	Me? What can *I* do? It's not my field!
Coach:	Yeah, but you're going to be playing on it in five minutes, and I need you to make some plays. (Reaffirm need to make decision)
Player:	I don't know. I can get down on the ball more, I guess.
Coach:	That will help. What else?
Player:	If I stay down low enough, I can always drop my knee to stop the ball if I have to.
Coach:	Sounds good. I know you can handle it. (Acknowledge decision)

PARENT TO CHILD

Child:	Mom, will you replace the ink cartridge in the printer?
Parent:	Why? What's wrong?
Child:	It's out of ink, and I have to print my paper.
Parent:	Sounds important! What are you going to do about it? (Push child to make decision)
Child:	Get you to change the cartridge!
Parent:	Can't do it now. The booklet for the printer is in the second drawer of the desk. There's a new cartridge there, too. Go for it!
Child:	I can't do this, Mom! (Knowing look from mother) OK! Where's the booklet?
Parent:	Second drawer in the desk. You'll do fine!

Connectedness Is Rewarding

Many of us are convinced that if we reward good behavior, we will see more of it. And, generally, we're right—on a short-term basis. Material reward works for a short time if the primary concern is to condition a particular behavior. When Tim gets five dollars a week to take out the garbage, he will become a world-class garbage taker-outer. But when mom or dad asks him to rake the back yard, his likely response is, "Hey, that wasn't a part of the deal!"

And it wasn't. We discover, then, that "what gets rewarded gets done." But we also discover that "what *doesn't* get rewarded doesn't get done." Not only did Tim's reward restrict the extent of his involvement around the house, but it actually prevented Tim from connecting with his parents' needs and with his own sense of responsibility.

The Best Rewards Are Inside Each of Us

Good coaches understand that the real value of a reward is found in its personal worth. Coaches reward leadership ability with opportunities to lead. They reward maturity with meaningful responsibility. They reward commitment with the opportunity to belong to a team with worthwhile and reachable goals. They reward hard work with specific recognition. I always gave recognition to the hardest-working kids during a brief meeting after practice. I was careful not to embarrass them; I just acknowledged their effort and used them as examples of what our team needed to be successful.

How do parents get kids to do what is rewarding, not just what gets rewarded? The answer is—recognize effort, not just accomplishment. Success is critical for every child. For that matter, it's critical for all of us. More important than the actual success, however, as desirable as it may be, is the effort that went into it. And when kids put effort into helping and connecting with others, when they shift the focus from me to you, their actions are rewarding.

Reward the Right Things

In other words, reward actions, not dreams. This is not to say that I didn't encourage kids to dream. It's just that I was careful to reward the here and now. What are you doing right now that will help your dreams come true? My job as a coach was not to push kids into a world of fantasy but to share their dreams by giving them the tools and promoting the effort to realize them. Dream of the future, but focus on the present.

Define success for your child in terms of "the good you do," not just "the good you get." When you teach your children to measure themselves by the good they do, they necessarily de-emphasize awards, grades, and money. This is not to say that awards and grades are unimportant. After all, they help define success. But imagine a family that taught youngsters to value themselves based on the good they did and to virtually disregard material things. In such a home, every child, even the most intellectually or athletically limited, could develop a strongly positive self-concept.

* * * * * * *

The dialoguing technique called "highlighting" can help do that. When you look for good deeds and regularly acknowledge them, you raise children who become self-fulfilling prophecies. Doing good becomes their standard of success. For you, it's simply a matter of watching for the right things.

Dialogue - Highlighting

COACH TO PLAYER

Coach:	Classy stuff, Carrie!
Player:	Huh? What do you mean?
Coach:	I like the way you picked that girl up after the foul. It was classy. (Highlighting with specific recognition)
Player:	Yeah, but I got a charging foul.
Coach:	Don't worry about it. That's going to happen! I just want to be able to count on you, and I just saw another reason why I can! (Focus on the good deed)

PARENT TO CHILD

Parent:	Kathleen, you just proved to me once again that real success is also about what you *don't* do!
Child:	What do you mean, Mom?
Parent:	You got one of the highest grades in your class on that history test, didn't you?
Child:	Yeah, I told you before dinner.
Parent:	Yes, but you hadn't told your dad yet, and you didn't tell him during dinner. (Highlighting with specific recognition)
Child:	Yeah, Dad and Danny were talking so much about Danny's problems in math, it just didn't seem like the right time.
Parent:	Yeah, Danny would have felt bad. But I sure was happy to see what you did. That grade is important to you. But your sensitivity for your little brother is just as important, maybe even more important. (Focus on the good deed)

Encouragement Creates Connectedness

The rigid taskmaster bellowing up and down the sidelines, bringing 300-pounders to their emotional knees, may survive as a marquee attraction, but he doesn't last long as a coach. Successful coaches have learned that shouting is for the stands, not the sidelines. Good-natured affection and encouragement create better relationships with players than bad-natured ranting and raving.

Many researchers have discovered that children from warm, caring homes are more self-controlled than children from harsh and punitive homes. They are more willing to confess misdeeds and often express genuine sadness when their behavior hurts someone else. By contrast, even when children from punitive homes are caught red-handed, they blame someone else for their actions and regret only one thing—being caught.

What coaches, teachers, and many parents have learned, therefore, is that punishment alone doesn't develop an adult-type conscience. Children from nonpunitive homes show much better development in this regard. Nor does punishment and excessive control develop character. Children in warm and loving families have stronger character development, and their self-control is more evident and more deeply rooted.

How Coaches Achieve Connectedness:

More Than Blind Obedience

Coaches have been known to lay down the law in no uncertain terms. They are connected enough with their kids to understand that young athletes must always operate within a clear framework of expectations. They also realize that kids sometimes need firmness. But good coaches realize that character development goes well beyond a blind obedience to rules. They don't want their athletes to simply fear punishment for rules violations. They want them to abide by rules because they understand them, accept and desire them, and have the self-discipline to want to follow them.

The more we cared about kids and connected with them, the more they cared about their own behavior. As kids came out to their first practice of the year, we always had the previous year's varsity players form a greeting line for the new players and welcome them. We also assigned one senior to every sophomore to be his big brother. When the season ended, we had next year's players line up and cheer the seniors as they left the practice field for the last time. The occasion was always marked by hugs, pats on the back, and more than a few tears.

Make a Pledge

That's why we asked our athletes to read and sign an Athlete's Pledge at the beginning of every football season. We wanted to be sure that they understood our expectations. We didn't throw the pledge in their faces every day. We simply shared it with them, discussed it, and asked them if they agreed with it. If they agreed, they were asked to sign it. If they didn't agree, we talked some more.

Then, as the season unfolded, we reminded them of the pledge whenever they used inappropriate language or failed to commit to team goals. Violations of the pledge often involved little more than a raised eyebrow. Once in a while, someone had to be punished with laps after practice or by apologizing to the team. Only once in my thirty-one-year career did we have to ask a young man to leave the team. It wasn't that we were reluctant to use such punishment; we just didn't have to. We all had connected with team expectations.

HOW PARENTS ACHIEVE CONNECTEDNESS:

Say It With Hugs

Demonstrated affection is far more powerful than a bunch of words. A hug doesn't take any time, and it has a powerful effect on kids. Hugs are like all-day suckers. Kids love to get them, they bring smiles, and they last until the kids go to bed at night.

I'm the first to believe in the power of "The Look." I've seen veteran teachers, usually women, freeze a misbehaving kid in his tracks with "The Look." I understand its power well; my wife has used it on me. "The Look" certainly has its place in every teacher's and parent's bag of disciplinary tricks. But parents must remember that a month of scowls pales before one momentary smile. The nurturing, nonpunitive home cultivates character development, whereas the harsh and over-controlling home is just one more obstacle in a child's growth toward happiness and self-reliance.

Expectations Are Helping Hands, Not Fists

The laissez-faire parent who avoids confrontation by providing little direction to kids is, in some ways, a bigger problem than the over-controlling parent. The relative absence of expectations may be harder on kids than expectations that are too rigid. Remember that your expectations should help children grow toward maturity. As such, they are helping hands that support growth, not fists that demand it.

* * * * * * *

The more often adolescents reflect on their behavior, the more they connect with others. Too many people in our society seem to be incapable of introspection. A coaching technique called reversing promotes empathy, and empathy promotes caring, concern, and a strong sense of moral responsibility. Asking kids what might happen if they *don't* behave in a certain way promotes such thinking.

Dialogue - Reversing

COACH TO PLAYER

Coach:	Tom, keep your arms above your head when getting ready to jump for a rebound. (Identify the need)
Player:	I just can't do it all the time. I like to use my arms to help me jump.
Coach:	I understand that. I was the same way. But what happens when you *don't* keep your arms above your head? (Use the reversing technique)
Player:	I feel I can jump higher!
Coach:	Is that what happened a couple nights ago—against that center from Fairfield? (Promote some thought)
Player:	Man, he sure crowded me, didn't he?
Coach:	Yes, he did, and what was the result?
Player:	I *couldn't* get my hands up.
Coach:	What would have been better—jumping a little higher or having your hands up to grab the ball?
Player:	OK, I'll work on it. (Commitment to different behavior)

PARENT TO CHILD

Parent:	John, do me a favor, would you? Try to stop the name-calling with your little brother. (Identify the need)
Child:	Then get him to stop being a dork.
Parent:	Well, he does some pretty childish things sometimes, but I don't think he's a dork.
Child:	I think he is. He's a pain.
Parent:	What would happen if you didn't call him names? (Use the reversing technique)
Child:	*I* sure wouldn't feel any better!
Parent:	Are you sure? What if your dad called you a dork? (Promote some thought)
Child:	I guess I'd get mad.

Parent: Maybe that's what happens with your brother.

Child: Yeah, I'm sure it does.

Parent: Do you think he'll probably react to you differently if he isn't mad? Kind of the way you'd react to your dad, who, by the way, doesn't call you a dork?

Child: Yeah, I guess so.

Parent: Will you try a little harder then?

Child: Yeah, OK. (Commitment to different behavior)

Unmet Needs = Unwanted Aggression

The need for affection or attention is a powerful motivator for kids. When the need is unmet, kids can sometimes turn to aggressive behavior to express their frustration. They may pick on a smaller child or, in the case of athletics, defy the coach, make a smart comment, or gesture inappropriately. When the parent or coach responds, the child has successfully gotten the attention he wanted. His need has been met, and his behavior has been reinforced.

I learned a long time ago that angry kids—including my own—will defy me. Psychologists tell us that they have to; it's a part of growing up. I also learned that if I overreacted, they won. They got exactly what they wanted. The most important thing I learned in this exchange is that the defiant comment is directed at "Coach" or "Dad," not at Mike. Because "Mike" wasn't pushed into the situation, I didn't take the defiance personally and was able to react less passionately.

Sometimes a strong reaction is required. Uncontrollable children require the services of everyone from school counselors or social workers to community youth officers or psychologists. But with most children an objective, dispassionate discussion works magic, especially if the coach or parent knows how to avoid being put on the defensive.

Take a Time Out

The defiance to coaches experience isn't always overt, and contrary to popular opinion, teenagers *can* be subtle. When athletes become defiant and disrupt practice, coaches maintain connectedness by using the equivalent of the nursery school's "time out": "Phil, take a lap and think about what you just did." Then, they proceed with practice and make a quick decision about how they'll handle Phil. In the sample dialogue which follows, the coach decided to take Phil aside and discuss the issue.

I kept three things in mind whenever I bumped into a Phil: One, I knew that when he finished running, I didn't want to be angry. Angry responses destroy connectedness. My life has been a recurring lesson that whenever I react in anger, I say stupid things. Saying stupid things disconnects us from kids and fails to influence their behavior. I wanted to stay connected. Two, I wanted to make sure that Phil didn't get the wrong kind of attention. The wrong kind of attention would reinforce the exact opposite of what I wanted from him.

Three—and this is a very important piece of information for parents and coaches—when Phil and I were done talking, I wanted to make sure that he was agreeing with me. I wanted him to nod his head or, better yet, smile. I knew that when we stopped talking, Phil's behavior—at that moment—was reinforced. If he was scowling, I just reinforced scowling. If he was mumbling defiance, that's what I reinforced. If he was nodding agreement, the agreement was reinforced. That's what I wanted.

Keep Your Cool

Taking the time to listen to kids or to give them an occasional hug works a world of miracles and can head off some defiant behavior. Many of us think that *we* motivate kids. Nothing is further from the truth. They already *are* motivated. The child's basic needs are his or her motivators. These basic needs must be satisfied; they *will* be satisfied one way or another. The question is, will we take the time to satisfy them positively, or will the child find negative satisfactions?

Reacting to kids in anger is like putting out to sea in a storm. It's hard to get to your destination, is rarely fun, and can be downright dangerous. Keep the waters calm. The journey is a whole lot smoother, and you'll guarantee that your child doesn't get exactly what he wanted, an upset mom or dad. Often, as in the dialogue, this is the perfect time to use "returning."

Don't take the anger personally. Recognize that your child is mad at Mom or Dad, that authority figure in the house. She's not mad at the inner you, just the outer boss. When I was a young coach, I once had a problem with one of my running backs. The angrier I got, the more surly he became. The head coach pulled me aside one day and said, "He's always had problems with authority. He's not surly with you, Mike. He's resenting his Coach, the authority figure on the field. He does the same thing with me. Don't take it so personally. Smile while you're holding his feet to the fire!" I dealt with the player more effectively almost immediately. I was able to think more clearly, and he suddenly discovered that he wasn't "getting to me."

At the moment the discussion or scolding stops, the child's behavior is reinforced. So be sure to promote the appropriate behavior before you stop the discussion. You can't do that when you're angry. It's also interesting to note an irony about the atmosphere in the harsh or punitive home. Inevitably, the threat of punishment or the harshness subsides, if only momentarily.

This reduction of threat provides for kids one of their most powerful kinds of reinforcement. Whatever they're doing at that moment will be reinforced, however undesirable it might be. Most important, we should recognize that inadvertent reinforcement of this type can easily be avoided if the atmosphere is positive to begin with.

* * * * * * *

Notice that the coach and the parent in the following dialogue don't allow the dialogue to end while the child is being defiant. The key is to "keep the ball in the child's court." That's why I call the technique "returning." It assures that the teen doesn't get the wrong kind of attention, and it helps parents maintain the composure to handle the situation correctly.

Dialogue - Returning

Coach: Phil, how many times have I told you not to use that kind of language out here?

Player: (Scowling) Lots!

Coach: Then why do you continue to do it? (Returning technique)

Player: What's the big deal? Everybody swears, and I get fed up sometimes. I guess it helps!

Coach: What does it help, Phil? (Returning technique)

Player: Me! I get a chance to blow!

Coach: And then you and I have this discussion. What would happen if you didn't swear? (Use the reversing technique)

Player: (Still scowling) I wouldn't be running as many laps, and I guess you and I wouldn't talk!

Coach: Is that right? Is swearing the only thing you and I ever talk about? (Returning technique)

Player: (Still scowling) OK. OK. I'll stop swearing.

Coach: Whoa, hold on, Phil. That doesn't sound very sincere. (Don't stop discussion while athlete is exhibiting negative behavior) I've always liked you, and I want to keep being able to trust you. Is trust important in our relationship? (Returning technique)

Player: Yeah, I guess it is.

Coach: Can I trust you then to try to stop swearing? (Returning technique)

Player: (Being more accepting) Yeah, OK, I'll try. (Good time to stop discussion)

PARENT TO CHILD

Child:	OK, Mom, let's go!
Parent:	Let's go where, honey?
Child:	Shopping! You said you'd take me today.
Parent:	I said I'd take you this morning, Peggy. It's one o'clock in the afternoon, and I have to make lasagna and clean the house. Your grandparents are coming later.
Child:	You do this to me all the time.
Parent:	What do I do to you all the time, Peg? (Returning technique)
Child:	Say we're gonna do something and then not do it.
Parent:	Excuse me, but exactly what did you say yesterday? (Returning)
Child:	To wake me up, and we'd go this morning.
Parent:	I woke you twice, you said "Yeah, Yeah," and went back to sleep.
Child:	So I was tired!
Parent:	Then maybe it's good you slept.
Child:	(Angry) Oh, great! Now how am I going to get those shoes? Just forget it!
Parent:	Wait a minute, Peg. It sounds like you're angry at *me*. Are you angry at *me*? (Don't stop discussion while child is exhibiting negative behavior)
Child:	I don't know. I guess not, but I need those shoes for the dance.
Parent:	What do you think you ought to do? (Returning technique and pushing technique)
Child:	I don't know. What *can* I do?
Parent:	There must be *some*thing. (Returning)
Child:	I guess I can call Cindy. Maybe she can drive.
Parent:	Good idea. Give it a try, but remember to be back in time to see your grandparents.
Child:	OK. (Good time to end discussion)

Let's Wrap It Up

Perhaps the best way to describe connectedness is to acknowledge that "We're all in this together." If our family, team, or organization is to be successful, we have to share common goals and to help each other achieve them. Connectedness is mutual caring and support. Psychologists tell us that kids must grow from a state of dependence to a state of independence. Such growth is essential. But they also must learn that they will never be completely independent.

To the contrary, kids must learn that they will always be completely *inter*dependent. We all are. We need each other to satisfy our needs, and children's needs are linked to others. Kids need to accomplish, to overcome failure, to accept blame, to impress others, and to give and receive help or sympathy. It's important for parents to recognize that the best way to help kids mature and develop character is to help them satisfy these needs.

Good coaches understand that athletes, like all kids, need role models and occasional inspiration, but that they are already powerfully motivated. I knew I was wasting my time if I spent most of it trying to motivate players. I also knew that if my players depended on me for motivation, they would also depend on me for control and for the reasons to make a maximum effort. Because they already were motivated to satisfy basic needs, my job was to help them. Their self-control and their effort would improve as these needs were satisfied.

Connectedness was critical. When introducing an offensive play to the backfield, for example, I emphasized that each player's job was important but that one of those jobs was critical. If the play involved a pass, the quarterback's job was critical. If it was a running play, the ball carrier's job was critical. In essence, it was the starring role. The other players in the backfield had supporting roles. They had to hand off the ball, fake, or block. Their roles, though less noticeable, were every bit as important if the play was to succeed.

Every sport has such supporting roles. Football refers to "running interference." Basketball has "assists." Baseball has the ultimate supporting role. They call it a "sacrifice." Families do the same things. Parents occasionally run interference for their kids. Siblings assist each other, and everyone sacrifices once in a while. Without such help, the needs of all family members are frustrated, and the family fails to realize its single most important purpose, everyone's happiness and positive growth.

John Wooden of UCLA, college basketball's greatest coach, emphasized a variation on this theme. He told all his players on the first day of practice never to criticize each other. Their jobs were supportive, to encourage each other as only teammates can. Wooden reasoned that players who receive ongoing encouragement and support believe in themselves, and players who believe in themselves perform better. Who can deny it? Children who believe in themselves perform better—in the classroom, on the athletic field, and at home. They also have character.

Parents are well-advised to borrow a page from Coach Wooden's book. Sometimes criticism is necessary, maybe even among siblings. But everyone in the family must remember that effective criticism provides light—not heat. Light reveals and illuminates. It shows the way. Heat, especially when it embarrasses kids, exhausts them and provokes anger and rebellion. It fails to satisfy needs and promote self-control, the subject of the next chapter.

2

CONTROL
It's What's Inside
That Counts

Character is impossible without self-control. Just watch television or read the paper, especially the sports page. The world of professional sport is populated by many athletes who are long on talent but short on character. A lot of them, in spite of their superior skills, find themselves traded more often than a kid's baseball cards. Their lack of self-control makes them about as dependable as a puppy's hind end. Coaches—at all levels—want dependability. Dependability that results from self-control builds great teams.

An early acquaintance of mine smiled when he heard I was a coach. "We just got a dog," he said, "and we named him 'Coach.'" Resigned to a friendly dig, I asked, "OK, why?" My friend said, "Because all he does all day is sit around and bark." After attempting a good-natured chuckle, I said, "That's funny, but it ain't no joke. There are more barkers out there than you think."

Maybe that's why I took such pride in one of my best coaching strategies. It promoted self-control and didn't involve barking. It indicated the level of self-control both my athletes and I had taken all season to achieve. Although it wasn't unique to me, I became good at it. I also used it in parenting my daughters. Maybe you use it, too.

It involved simple eye contact and the hundreds of words that fill one moment of nonverbal communication. Coaches learn all too soon that the heat of battle is not the time to correct something wrong or even recognize something good.

When Tom drops the ball on the five yard line, coaches don't have time to sit down and chat. Eye contact has to say it all.

I'm not talking about "The Look." "The Look" is designed to get kids to stop whatever it is they're doing. It is one-way communication designed to freeze junior in midstep. It assumes that the child needs external control. The strategy I'm referring to is "The Link." It assumes that the athlete is internally controlled, that he *already* has looked at his behavior and that he's ready to improve his performance or be congratulated. It is two-way communication. It is my communication to the child that "I saw that," his communication to me that "I did, too, and I'm going to do something about it."

A self-controlled athlete who makes a mistake knows that I'm watching, and he's probably not in the mood for criticism. He simply wants me to know that *he* knows. And, frankly, that's good enough for me. I want him to be self-aware and self-critical. After all, that's what self-discipline is. Like motivation, discipline is not what I do; it's what my kids do. I want them to be self-critical, even when we don't make eye contact—even when I'm not around.

Parents want the same thing. Obviously, "The Link" can be effective only after athletes understand and accept what is expected of them. They have to know the right way to perform, then judge their performance accordingly. This assumes that I've done a good job teaching the expectations and creating the kind of relationship that inspires their willingness to judge their performance. Without such self-evaluation, self-control is impossible.

Self-control is one of the hallmarks of character. Without it, children never develop the internal discipline that promotes the other facets of character. It's the best kind of discipline. External discipline, especially in the form of punishment, is necessary only after a child's self-control breaks down.

Self-Control Starts With You

We have to control our own motivations before we can hope to promote self-control in our children. Looking at our own motivations involves some pretty serious soul-searching, but we'd better do it if we hope to connect enough with our kids to influence their character development. We've all had that feeling that we're going to explode if we don't say something. I've learned that's almost always the best time to say nothing.

As a coach, I've learned to ask myself a couple important questions: "Whose needs am I satisfying—my players' or mine?" "Is winning more important to me than working with my athletes?" Whenever winning becomes more important than working with kids, coaches and kids lose perspective. At such times, coaches also lose a source of enjoyment and perhaps their biggest reason for going into coaching in the first place. When kids become faceless pawns in a desperate need to win, everyone loses.

Children will never learn self-control from someone who has none. Smart coaches know that they can't control their surroundings unless they first control themselves. With such control comes the ability to resolve conflicts, not to become a part of them.

Effective coaches are also good models. They work hard, cooperate with their players and fellow coaches, promote mutual respect, and use appropriate language. I learned long ago that nothing is more embarrassing than suddenly seeing a youngster imitate a stupid behavior of mine. On the other hand, nothing is more complimentary than watching a player imitate my good behavior. It's also character-building for the player.

Ask yourself similar questions. Is my child's behavior and attitude suggesting that I might be over-involved? Am I pushing a little too hard? Do I lose my self-control when I'm in the stands, on the sidelines, or in the audience? Does my desire for her to be on the Student Council contribute more to my ego than to hers? Is an A his accomplishment or mine? If the answers to the above questions focus on your needs more than your child's, back off!

Depersonalize the Situation

When conflicts arise, talk about behaviors, not people. Tim is not the cause of your anger or shame; his behavior is. Focus on the real problem. And above all, know what pushes your buttons; don't allow yourself to lose your self-control and to be drawn into a problem for all the wrong reasons. Philosopher Kahlil Gibran advised: "Let there be spaces in our togetherness."

This means that you know when to walk away. When coaches need time to think, they call a time-out. Call time-outs. A wise father once told his son, "Never pass up the opportunity to keep your mouth shut." There comes a time in any discussion, no matter how right you think you are, when keeping your mouth shut is your best response.

Focus on the Issues at Hand

Control your body language, the tone and speed of your own language. Sometimes our actions are so loud, no one can hear what we say. And don't allow past circumstances to influence the current situation. Focus on the issues at hand. Tom's lousy report card last year is not something to throw in his face because of one poor grade this year. My job as a coach is to help kids focus completely on the present moment. I know that they'll never perform well now if they dwell on past mistakes. So don't remind kids of past mistakes: "You shoulda done this" produces negative self-talk. Rather, say, "Do *right now* what you can do."

Conserve Your Energy

Coaches wouldn't be involved in athletics if they didn't like a good battle once in a while. But good coaches, like good parents, understand that they have only so much energy, and they learn to conserve it. They learn, for example, that sometimes it's wiser to avoid a conflict than to resolve one. The time and effort taken to connect with kids and to promote their self-control provides immediate and long-range benefits. It's better to have your kids turn to you for advice than away from you for relief.

The possibility of an angry response suggests another important point. Your ire may add just the right amount of spice to your position, but too much of it creates the wrong effect. The parent who gets angry at trivial misbehaviors should ask himself the question, "Is this the hill I want to die on?" Is this issue important enough to warrant all this energy and negativity?

* * * * * * *

Standing back from the problem, separating from it, is always a good idea. The parent who counts to ten models the essence of self-control to his or her child. Children learn to control their tempers when they see mom controlling hers. "Separating" is a great dialoguing technique to model such behavior.

Dialogue - Separating

COACH TO PLAYER

Player:	This play sucks!
Coach:	(Coach takes a deep breath, then . . .) Whoa, Fred; slow down. We're having our problems, but this play is *going to work* against Deerfield.
Player:	You can't even make it work here!
Coach:	(After about five or six seconds of silence) Slow down a minute and think about what you're saying. Our plays have been working all year. This will too.
Player:	Yeah, well, I'm not about to. . . .
Coach:	(Without raising his voice but holding up his hand) OK, hold it; you're about to say some things you don't mean and that might cause you and me a problem or two. Let's get back to the issue. (Coach separates from personal nature of disagreement)
Player:	Well, I. . . .
Coach:	(Again interrupting) Let's give the play fifteen more minutes of hard work, and then I'll want to hear what you and everyone else has to say about the play. Fair? (Refocus on issue and maintain separation.)
Player:	Yeah, I guess. . . .
Coach:	(Quickly) Then let's get back to work.

PARENT TO CHILD

Child:	What do you mean I can't sleep over at Tammy's after the Homecoming Dance?
Parent:	Honey, most of those kids are seniors. You're a freshman.
Child:	So what? I know what I'm doing.
Parent:	Yes, you're very responsible, but you're going to have to trust me on this one. Sometimes. . . .

Child:	(Interrupting) I hate you when you treat me like this!
Parent:	(After six or seven seconds of silence) That's a little extreme, honey. Fortunately, I know you don't mean it. You're just mad. (Separation technique) Let's get back to the issue. (Refocus on the situation)
Child:	The issue is that you're mean and you treat me like a child.
Parent:	(Ignoring comment about being "mean") Maybe that's what it seems like, but let's talk about maturity and fifteen-year-old girls. . . . (Remain focused on the issue and maintain separation)

Hey! No one ever said that these dialoguing techniques were easy. As indicated in this last example, being the adult is quite a challenge. But unless someone is the adult in such a discussion, nothing much will be accomplished. In fact, much damage can be done. It's also important to note that sometimes a more rigorous consequence is needed if the child won't back off. Normally, however, if we keep our cool—they'll find theirs.

Nurturing Self-Control

If discipline is necessary, consider the philosophy of one of history's greatest coaches. Former UCLA coach John Wooden's philosophy of discipline is uncomplicated: "Make the rules clear and the penalties severe." His definition of severity had nothing to do with physical or emotional abuse. Wooden vigorously opposed such treatment of kids and young adults. He meant simply to assure that the kids understand the rules, that the punishment fit the crime, and that kids understand that the consequences of misbehavior simply aren't worth the risk.

How Coaches Teach Self-Control:

Character Is a Black and White Issue

Coach Wooden was also quick to point out that hard work, consideration, respect for others, honesty, and integrity are black and white. There are no gray areas when it comes to these kinds of issues. Coaches don't bargain about hard work, commitment, teamwork, and consideration. These are the building blocks of character. Coaches realize that kids need and want boundaries, so coaches establish reasonable expectations, sometimes collaboratively with athletes and their parents. Then, they stick to them, remembering that youngsters need and *want* a clear sense of direction. Indecision interferes with self-control. Good coaches don't permit such indecision.

Make the Expectations Clear

Clear expectations eliminate indecision. Good coaches don't want athletes wondering or rationalizing about the "right" thing to do. They want them to *know* the right thing to do—then *do* it. Then, if they don't do it, the consequences may be severe or they may be light, but they are always immediate—or as immediate as coaches can make them. Usually, they are simple reminders, less often punishments.

Mind Your Manners

Emphasizing good manners is one of the simplest ways to teach self-control. Effective coaches emphasize manners all the time: "Don't swear!" "Help your opponent off the ground!" "Act like young men/young women when we travel to an 'away' game." "Whenever you answer me, answer 'Yes, coach' or 'Yes, ma'am'!" Most young athletes abide by such expectations. They even enjoy them, especially when they feel connected with the coach.

How Parents Teach Self-Control:

What Do You Think?
Coaches often ask athletes and their parents for input regarding the development or modification of training rules and the Athletic Code. Similarly, parents should ask children for their input regarding family rules and consequences. Such dialogue encourages kids to think about the "what" and "why" behind appropriate behavior. Considerate behavior doesn't just *happen*; it involves genuine learning, and parents are the best teachers. Having dialogued about family rules, children are more likely to develop the self-control to follow the rules, or at least to understand the consequences if they don't.

Don't Set the Bar Too High
If the rules are too demanding, kids become frustrated. Then, they act out their frustrations and misbehave; their self-control breaks down. Rigid control in the home is restrictive. Good discipline involves expectations but within a nurturing environment. Parents must never forget that the expectations we impose on our children provide the framework within which they find their successes.
When the only standard of success is superior achievement, we send the wrong message. Consider the message sent by the International Olympic Committee (IOC) in the '80s and '90s when they allowed professionals to compete in the Olympics. Sport for its own sake gave way to the desire to win. When anything for its own sake gives way to the desire to "win," kids learn the wrong lessons.

Reasons, Not Excuses
Misbehavior often involves a lot of reasons but never an excuse. "I forgot" or "I didn't mean it" are never acceptable.

These are cop-outs. "I forgot!" is not an excuse but a *reason* for misbehavior or an error in judgment and, as such, should be regarded as an admission of wrongdoing. Parents must not simply "OK" it. All that does is encourage more forgetting or poor judgment in the child.

Children who learn that excuses don't work begin to govern their behavior more carefully. They also learn to accept the boundaries imposed by reasonable expectations. Kids with no boundaries lose their way and inevitably make bad decisions. Kids not only want boundaries, they want a sense of direction, a predictability that smoothes over those rough spots on the way to adulthood.

You Goofed? Raise Your Hand

Simple fear and avoidance of punishment is childish. Help your adolescents realize consequences when they misbehave. The more consistently the consequences are experienced, the more aware children are of appropriate behavior and the more likely they are to be self-controlled.

And be sure that the consequences fit the crime. Severe consequences for simple misbehavior teach kids to lie about their actions and to try to escape punishment. A fear and avoidance of consequences may be childish and yet another reason to emphasize character with your kids, but it might also result from an extreme reaction to their behavior. We have to consider our own behavior as well as theirs when emphasizing character development.

There's a Right Way and a Wrong Way

Effective parents teach manners, too: "Don't slurp your soup." "Watch your language!" "Ask to be excused from the table." "Can you say 'thank you'?" Parents who are already adept at teaching character recognize that expecting good manners is the first step in teaching self-control. They also know that "The Link" is an effective strategy. It shows that someone is watching, even at the dinner table. The child who controls his behavior at the dinner table or among family friends controls his behavior elsewhere.

Be realistic. Make sure you expect from the situation only what is realistic. Above all, be realistic about what you can and cannot resolve. A veteran coach once told me to distinguish between problems and dilemmas. He believed that problems could be resolved; dilemmas couldn't. Dilemmas required that the situation simply be made more comfortable for everyone involved.

Dilemmas generally are beyond our control. The coach can solve his personnel problem by switching players or by changing the offense to match the skills of his current crop of athletes. He cannot resolve the dilemma of gusting winds on game day. Nor can he completely eliminate the occasional ill will felt by two kids who are working hard for the same position. He can only acknowledge and accept the circumstances and encourage the players to overcome them.

Similarly, parents can resolve the problem of their son's misbehavior by dialoguing with him or by taking away the car keys. They cannot resolve the periodic dilemma of his raging adolescence. Adolescent hormones introduce moments of irrationality that can leave parents and others slack-jawed. At such times, parents can only acknowledge the circumstances and help everyone in the family deal with them—as openly and as unemotionally as possible.

Watch Out for the Sunshine Syndrome

Being open means that we recognize that the world is not bright and cheery all the time. We can't allow our desire for a rational and happy world to blind us to reality. Sports teams and families are not always rational! Retreating into a state of false contentment is self-defeating. Sometimes kids cause problems; sometimes they lose their self-control. When they do, don't be so overwhelmed by the confusion that you fail to act.

When children misbehave, never retreat into a state of nothingness, simply pretending that all is well. All is *not* always well, and children and parents are *not* always wonderful. The Sunshine Syndrome can both bind and blind. It can promote a sense of family that binds people together, yet it can blind family members to each other's faults and misbehaviors. Self-control requires self-criticism. A laissez-faire attitude will never help children develop self-control.

Parents Fail Too

Sometimes a child's self-control fails. And sometimes a parent fails by not knowing how to react. We know a laissez-faire attitude is wrong, but we don't know what corrective action to take. This sense of failure, as uncomfortable as it might be, should never get in the way of some kind of response.

We are far more influential in the lives of our children than we realize. This awareness alone should cause us to intervene. A child's positive behavior and learned self-control are far more important than our feelings of success or failure. We are rarely wrong when we positively confront children when they misbehave. I thank heaven my mother had the courage to risk my anger when she corrected my misbehavior.

* * * * * * *

Let's for the moment recognize one of life's lessons. We have all experienced a variety of "non-negotiables" that society and our physical worlds impose on us. They don't involve any gray areas. These are not issues or situations that involve good arguments on both sides. They are black and white, one-sided expectations that stand firmly on their own merits. They may range from not hurting ourselves by playing with fire to not hurting others by being inconsiderate and abusive.

Coaches impose similar expectations. Coach John Wooden provides another excellent example. He imposed the expectation on all his players that basketball practice involves nothing but a maximum and focused effort. Wooden told his players that no matter what was happening in their personal lives, when they hit the practice court, they were there to play basketball. If a parent was ill, Wooden offered to meet with the player at the player's convenience, but even a parent's illness was not allowed to interfere with the player's focus on basketball.

Sounds a little extreme and uncaring, doesn't it? But consider what it does. It teaches youngsters to put their problems into separate boxes to be handled at the right time. Such ability enables them to concentrate on other important responsibilities as well, in other words to handle *all* the elements of their lives as adults. Tragedy, as overwhelming as it is, requires our complete focus, but so do the other responsibilities in our lives.

It is these other responsibilities, when disregarded, that can magnify *all* our problems. There is a best time and place to handle each of our responsibilities. Youngsters must learn this lesson in order to handle everything life throws at them. More will be said of this in a future chapter. For now, "Expecting" is an excellent dialoguing technique to promote this behavior.

Dialogue - Expecting

COACH TO PLAYER

Coach: Tom, what's happening today? Your mind is somewhere else.

Player: I found out from my counselor today that I can't get into Yale. I really wanted Yale.

Coach: Yes, I know you did. I'm sorry to hear that.

Player: So I guess I'm not with it, Coach.

Coach: Well, I'll tell you, Tom. I want you to *get* with it. I need you and your teammates need you. This is a big game this weekend.

Player: Hey, I'm just down. Can't you understand that?

Coach: I sure do—and I don't blame you. You and I will have a long talk about that after practice. (Help Tom put his problem in a separate box) I'm sure we'll be able to come up with something. You're a pretty resilient guy, but in the meantime, we need your complete attention and a maximum effort from you right now. (Impose current expectations)

Player: I'm just not sure I can do that.

Coach: Yes, you can—and you will. We're all here to help you. Come on, show me all that good stuff you're made of. (Coach provides encouragement and help but persists with the non-negotiability of the expectation. Coach also allows no room for anything else.)

PARENT TO CHILD

Parent: Carrie, isn't it about time to study some more for your finals? You're only two days away.

Child: I just got off the phone with Tom. He broke up with me.

Parent:	Aw, honey, that's too bad. You two were seeing each other for a long time.
Child:	Yeah, I can't study just now. I can't even think straight.
Parent:	OK, Carrie, let's talk. (Mom talks to Carrie for more than an hour to empathize with her. Sometimes feelings are more important than non-negotiables.)
Child:	Thanks, Mom. You really do understand how I feel.
Parent:	Well, as I pointed out, breaking up is a problem we all run into at one time or another.
Child:	Yeah, I guess.
Parent:	Do you know what else I know?
Child:	What?
Parent:	That you have finals in two days and that you have to study for them. (Reintroduce the non-negotiability of studying for finals)
Child:	I don't know how I can.
Parent:	Just take them one at a time, honey. (Stick to the expectations) You might even discover that they get your mind off Tom. Go ahead; give it a try. (Re-emphasize non-negotiability and leave room for nothing else)

Show Some Spirit

Kids are incredibly spontaneous, sometimes over-exuberant. Helping our kids develop self-control doesn't mean we don't *want* them to be spontaneous; a zest for living is a sure sign of character. Spirit is the energy that drives families as well as teams. It also involves risk-taking and, because it does, occasionally requires behaviors that compromise self-control. The child who is willing to take risks, to step out on the edge of whatever is secure and safe, can also be the child who challenges our tolerance levels. Good coaches and good parents understand that.

Give It a Try

Good coaches understand that when youngsters are pushed out of their safe zones, their behavior may change. They may get a little too sober or a little too silly. Either way, the smart coach tolerates the change. He knows that the apparent loss of self-control won't last forever. Obviously, if the unwanted behavior continues, the coach corrects it. But usually, the good coach accepts the behavior as the child's spirited attempt to try something new.

"You can do it!" is one of the most encouraging things anyone can say to a child. This is one of the best ways to help kids realize their goals. Coaches say, "Go for it!" They usually add one of two other demands: "Expect to win!" or "Refuse to lose!" Such positive self-talk often creates self-fulfilling prophecies; some youngsters may not have the ability to win but eventually do because they are self-controlled and confident enough to believe they can.

Test Your Limits

Coaches encourage athletes to test their limits, to get out of their safe zones in order to risk failure. Parents must do the same thing. Encourage your kids to try out for the cheerleading squad, to run for the Student Council, to take the tougher course. Parents must help children learn from their failures; more important, they must learn that they can fail at a task without *being* a failure.

All of us have a gremlin, that little creature somewhere in the back of our heads that tells us not to take chances. Gremlins like the status quo. They don't want to try anything new. In fact, they insist that we'll fail if we try something new. Youngsters have to learn how to recognize, then fight their gremlins. They'll need your help whenever they do it. Introduce them to their gremlins and then address the gremlin directly when the child falters in the face of a new task: "You don't want to try out for basketball? Let's talk to your gremlin. What's he saying?" "That accelerated course in math has you a little shook up, doesn't it? What's your gremlin telling you?"

Show Some Excitement

Good coaches and parents get excited when kids beat their gremlins. They also understand that such children sometimes get too excited. They behave or speak inappropriately; they go too far. They may get a little cocky, or their energy levels may provoke misbehavior. Handle such misbehavior as a failed task. Help the child learn from it, and do it with good humor. An angry response may simply teach the child to stop taking risks.

Trivial misbehaviors are the best opportunities for "The Link." Establish the unspoken communication to determine if you and your child are on the same wave length. If you are, he will exercise more self-control. But this requires diligence on your part. Always watch for opportunities. One link doesn't make a chain. A succession of links creates a strong and effective relationship with your child.

A Pat on the Back Is Better Than a Kick in the Slats

Be vigilant. Connect with your kids. Don't just react to bad behavior; recognize good behavior. When you start "catching 'em being *good*," you'll discover that they won't be bad as often, that their self-control will improve. Recognize and applaud the opinions and the ideas of your children. Help them develop realistic and worthwhile goals. Your children will relate to you more comfortably, and they'll have the self-control and the confidence to take risks because they'll know that they won't get hurt when they do.

* * * * * * *

Boosting is an important dialoguing technique because it enables you to encourage your children when they question their abilities. When boosting your child, be a coach, not a cheerleader. Specifically recognize your child's skills; in essence, remind her of what she probably already knows. When you simply praise her and she knows the praise is undeserved, not only will the effects of the boosting be lost on her, but your credibility will suffer.

Boosting is an opportunity for you to remind your child that you believe in him, that he has resources that will work for him, and that you are always available for love and support. "You're one of my most committed players. I know if you dig just a little deeper, you can perfect that block." "The game looks a little bleak, doesn't it? Dip into that big well of character that made you one of the best leaders I've ever had and help get us over the hump!" "Honey, you've proven your math ability for years. Learn what you can from that low test score, then do what you know you can do. Jump all over the next test!"

Dialogue - Boosting

Player: Coach, you know I'm trying, but that guy is beating me to death. I feel like a blocking dummy; he's doing anything he wants with me.

Coach: We knew going in that he was good—and he is. But so are you. (Boosting technique) You're not the biggest, but you're one of the toughest defensive tackles I've ever coached. (More boosting)

Player: Yeah, well tough ain't getting it done today.

Coach: OK, but smart will. You've got great technique, Tom. (Specifically recognize his skills) Use it.

Player: What do you mean?

Coach: Don't muscle with him. Get underneath his block. Submarine him, the way you did last year against Samuels, remember? (More specific recognition)

Player: Yeah, sometimes we just made a big pile in the hole. I got so low, he couldn't move me.

Coach: Do the same thing to this guy. Make a believer of him. Remind him that he's playing against one of the best defensive tackles in the conference. (More boosting)

Player: Yeah. Thanks, Coach. Let's do it.

PARENT TO CHILD

Child: I don't know about accelerated English, Mom. Maybe I should register for the regular class.

Parent: Why, honey? You've been getting straight As in English since your freshman year. (Boosting technique) Two of your teachers recommended you for the course.

	Let's talk to your gremlin for a minute. What's he telling you?
Child:	Well, for one thing, he's reminding me that Junior English has more reading and a term paper.
Parent:	So what are you going to tell him?
Child:	I guess I could remind him that I always get good grades on my papers.
Parent:	I think you're right! He forgets that your greatest strength is writing. (Specific recognition of strengths and more boosting) That term paper will be a great chance to show this next teacher what you've got!
Child:	Yeah, maybe you're right. I really do like to write.
Parent:	Of course you do. You're good at it. We all like to do things we're good at! (More boosting) Tell your gremlin to back off.
Child:	OK, mom—thanks. Let's go for it.

Check Their Fundamentals

Some kids are developmentally unable to do some of the things coaches and parents want them to do. They just need more time to "grow up" before they can demonstrate the self-control we want from them. That parents and coaches recognize this is very important.

Are They Ready?

Coaches must determine if kids are physically ready to perform certain skills. If my quarterback can throw the ball only thirty-five yards with accuracy, I'd better keep all my pass plays short, and I'd better try to develop a strong running game. It's easier for a quarterback to maintain self-control when he's working within the range of his abilities.

Similarly, coaches must be aware of players' emotional skills. If my recent move-in is surly most of the time and seems unable to make friends, I'd better take the time to find out what's wrong. If not, he won't enjoy his experience, and the team may not get to capitalize on his skills if he fails to adjust. Something's going on with him. The quicker I find out, the more self-control he will develop and the happier everyone will be.

Some children are developmentally unable to accept others as individuals in their own right. Young children tend to be self-absorbed and very concrete when they look at themselves in relation to the rest of the world. They're downright selfish. Child psychologists tell us that such behaviors are normal. Only with maturation do kids achieve the ability to abstract. Until they can think in abstract terms, they are unable to accept the feelings of others as real.

They tend to abide by rules because they fear punishment or an upset mom or dad. They focus on what will happen to them, not on what their behavior does to others. Their self-control, then, has little to do with the feelings of others. This tendency can last longer in some children than in others. Parents are wise to remember that their children might not yet be ready to learn about increased risk-taking, cooperation, or competition. Self-control is still at its rudimentary stages and may not develop significantly until the child matures.

Consider the Bigger Needs Too

In sports, kids must develop fundamental skills, but they also have fundamental needs. Fair treatment is one of those needs. It's those times when they *aren't* treated fairly, when they sense injustice, when they feel rejected—when their fundamental needs are thwarted—that problems arise. These are the times when kids lose self-control. Famed psychologist Abraham Maslow believed that the persistent denial of truth, justice, or beauty makes people sick, actually *sick*. The sickness may be physical or psychological, but it's always serious enough to negatively influence behavior, especially self-control. People denied truth become paranoid; people denied justice become rebellious; people denied beauty become depressed, sometimes violent.

Our job as parents and coaches is to guarantee these fundamentals. Even if a child lives in an economically depressed area and experiences injustice or ugliness on the streets, the parents can provide justice and beauty in the home. Many struggling parents do exactly this for their children, and their children find reasons to succeed and to develop self-control, even in the most trying social circumstances.

I Don't Want Great; I Want Good

There's a switch. Of course, coaches want great. They want great effort, great commitment, and great consistency. Many of them want great performances. As indicated throughout this book, however, the coaches who demand great effort know that great performances will follow, at least good enough performances. Parents want the same thing, great effort, especially when it comes to *doing* good! Great effort is possible for every child who seeks to do good, and it avoids the frustration that sometimes makes self-control so difficult.

Telling kids that they're "the greatest" is fun, surprisingly easy, and invariably true when we expect them to be the greatest at being good, especially at *doing* good. Chapter One made the point that even the most intellectually or athletically limited kid can *do* good, and if doing good is his standard for success, he can be as successful as his effort will allow. Strong self-concepts result from successes. Help your child define success as reaching out to others, and you help him feel good about himself, become self-controlled, and develop character. Review the dialoguing technique "Boosting."

Let's Wrap It Up

Sometimes good coaches rethink their goals for the season. Injuries, different opponents, and new kids in key positions provoke offensive and defensive adjustments. Changing circumstances cause us to change or slightly adjust our purposes. Parents, coaches, teachers, and every other fair-thinking person in our society must take the time to rethink or reaffirm our goals for kids in this new millennium. To promote self-control in our children, homes, schools, and communities we must teach them to:

- Develop social skills.
- Identify ways to relate to society's institutions.
- Learn how to exert positive influence in a democratic society.
- Explore their personal strengths and weaknesses.
- Understand the increasing interdependence within our society.
- Explore the what and why of our responsibilities to other people.
- Understand the differences between wants and needs.
- Practice decision making as it relates to values, attitudes, and reasoning.
- Take risks in the face of uncertainty.
- Appreciate the moral and social value of hard work.

Good coaches look beyond Xs and Os to develop the total athlete. Similarly, schools must look beyond purely academic curricula to develop the total student. Understanding such principles of behavior will provoke the kind of consistency kids need to develop character. These are desirable principles, unlike some of the practices perpetuated by our society. Television, movies, and music at times seem to conspire against parents and teachers, many of whom fail to acknowledge the importance of the above ideas.

Children can master these principles, particularly when their ego and social needs are satisfied. Little children tend to misbehave when their *wants* are unmet. Older children misbehave when their *needs* are unsatisfied, when they are denied food or a sense of belonging, security, recognition, or competence. Children who are loved and who have a solid sense of self may get out of line once in a while, but they tend to be more self-disciplined than neglected children. They are also open to new learning experiences. A consistency of treatment leads to a consistency of behavior, the focus of the Chapter Four.

3

COMMITMENT
Promoting Strong Wills and Weak Won'ts

Commitment is an eighty-pound gymnast doing three back walkovers and nailing her dismount. It's an average English student burning the midnight oil every evening to get an A on his final exam. It's an ordinary-type kid who does extraordinary things because she understands how to dedicate herself to a task.

Quite simply, a commitment is a pledge to yourself or to someone else to do something—to *really* do something. Sometimes, we agree to a certain action but feel little obligation to follow through. If we get around to it, fine. If not, so what? At other times, we're compelled to make decisions. But such decisions may involve nothing more than choosing between the marinara or the Alfredo sauce. Commitments go well beyond such simple agreements or decisions. They involve a pledge and a course of action from which there is no turning back.

Because commitments involve strong ties to a course of action, they often relate to one or more passions in our lives. At such times, commitments happen naturally. Michael Jordan was committed to basketball. Why wouldn't he be? It was his whole life. My grandfather, Jim Thorpe, was committed to athletics. Why not? It defined who he was and ultimately provided a standard of living he never would have found on his Indian allotment back in Oklahoma. Commitment is easy under such circumstances.

Securing commitments from youngsters is more difficult if they have no passion for the task. Getting them to commit to a sport they like only incidentally or to homework in subjects they may actually dislike is a continuing challenge for coaches and parents. Fortunately, there are several things we can do. The first of these identifies the characteristics of tasks or activities to which most kids seem willing to commit.

What Kids *Want* to Commit To

Consider this: more than half the youngsters involved in organized sports quit before their teens. They say the sport is no longer fun or they just don't enjoy it anymore. Thousands of kids are quitting every year because some adults have organized the fun right out of sports. In fact, some kids quit when games become sports, when kids become athletes, and when parents become fans. Some of them discover that the fun found in "games" surrenders to the occasional abuses found in "sports."

They meet inexperienced coaches who never "entered the arena." They never felt the pain or shed the tears that sometimes accompany a total commitment. Some of these coaches compensate for their own failure as players by becoming "tough guys" as coaches. They misinterpret the philosophies of great coaches like Lombardi by berating kids and by driving them too hard. When play becomes just hard work, it loses its appeal, and kids refuse to commit to sports that fail to satisfy them.

Unfortunately, some families do much the same thing. Some parents find vicarious success in the accomplishments of their children. Certainly, this is not all bad. Good parents smile when their teen brings home an A or makes the traveling team. They are proud of their child and, let's admit it, more than a little proud of their influence on him or her. But when some parents, like some unprincipled coaches, push their kids too hard to satisfy their own need for success, the child and his or her needs are obscured. A result is a child who either quits or fails to make the total commitment his school work and sport requires.

Raising kids involves one fine line after another. One of those fine lines finds us wondering if we're pushing our kids too much or not enough. But that's OK. We can fall over this line once in a while. We're going to make an occasional mistake and push a little too hard, but we're also going to have the sensitivity to recognize our mistakes, talk to the child, and back off. The problem for children comes when some parents fail to recognize their own motivations and stay on the wrong side of the line.

* * * * * * *

When we feel the need to push and we want to stay on the right side of the line, the dialoguing strategy called "Looking Inside" helps kids focus on the needs they want to satisfy. Sometimes the circumstances of their involvement obscure what they want from the experience, and it ceases to satisfy them or to be fun. We have to help them look inside at such times to rediscover their goals and to find the best ways to reach them.

Dialogue - Looking Inside

COACH TO PLAYER

Coach:	OK, Mary, let's take a minute or two to talk.
Player:	Why? What's going on?
Coach:	Your mind seems to be in a different place half the time. What's distracting you from having a good time out here? (Seek to identify the problem)
Player:	I don't know. Maybe it's these crazy turnovers. I feel like I can't even handle the ball anymore.
Coach:	Yes, you have been having a problem compared to last year. What's different this year? (Get athlete to look at the situation carefully)
Player:	I don't know.
Coach:	Well, what happened last year when you weren't turning the ball over? (Probe for more self-analysis)
Player:	I just handled the ball, drove to the basket, and made assists.
Coach:	Well, why would this year be any different? (Encourage comparison and contrast)
Player:	I feel like the whole team is looking to me for leadership. I guess I just feel more pressure.
Coach:	Understandable. You're one of the captains and a three-year starter. That's causing a little pressure, huh? (Establish rapport by acknowledging the athlete's concerns)
Player:	I guess it is. What do I do?
Coach:	No easy answers, kid, but I'll tell you what *we* can do. (Promote more looking inside by avoiding simple solutions. This is only incidentally your problem. The athlete has to solve it by looking inside.)

Player: What?

Coach: We're going to talk some more tomorrow, and in the meantime, I want you to answer this question for yourself: "What do I have to do to make this job easier for me and to have more fun?" Same time, same place tomorrow? (Provoke more looking inside by asking another important question)

Player: OK, Coach.

PARENT TO CHILD

Parent: Hey, Sal, you got a minute?

Child: Yeah, I guess. What's up?

Parent: It's this telephone. I can actually pick it up without burning my hand. Why no calls lately?

Child: Oh, just stuff, I guess.

Parent: Stuff? What kind of stuff? (Seek to identify the problem)

Child: I just don't know about some of my friends. They're changing—or maybe I am.

Parent: What seems to be changing? Any specifics? (Get the child to look at the situation carefully)

Child: I guess I've been pulling back. (Hesitation) Pot. One of the specifics is pot.

Parent: Talk to me about it. How do you see it? (Probe for more self-analysis)

Child: No one ever used it before. Now some of my friends are using a lot.

Parent: Yeah, and that's bothering you because you know it's wrong. Maybe you're even finding yourself a little tempted. (Establish rapport by acknowledging child's concerns)

Child: Yeah, I guess so, and I know how *you* feel about that!

Parent:	You're right about that, but guess what? How I feel about it isn't as important as how *you* feel about it. (This is only secondarily your problem. The child has to solve it by looking inside.)
Child:	Well, what do I do about *that*?
Parent:	That's a tough one, Sal. There are no easy answers, but I'll tell you what we can do. (Promote more looking inside by avoiding simple solutions)
Child:	What?
Parent:	Let's talk some more tomorrow. Between now and then, I want you to think about this question: "What am I willing to change about my relationship with my friends?" Tomorrow?
Child:	OK, Mom.

We all need to refocus once in a while on the qualities we seek in certain activities. We also have to look at our own behavior in relation to them. Most of these qualities relate to the satisfaction of our needs and are very important to us. If coaches and parents emphasize these needs in their activities and at home, children are more likely to make the commitments that lead to success as well as to character development. They also are more likely to adjust their own behavior at times and to be willing to open up to mom and dad—a great fringe benefit. Let's look at a few, first from the perspective of coaches.

HOW COACHES TEACH COMMITMENT:

Kids Need Something to Commit To

Not having anything to feel important about causes more emotional emptiness in kids and in many adults than a lack of anything else in our lives. Good coaches understand this and give young athletes causes beyond themselves to identify with and to believe in. Hard work, a total commitment to personal and team excellence, opportunities for self-sacrifice, and genuine caring for each other are qualities to believe in. They also give kids purposes which are greater than themselves. Nothing is really worthwhile unless we have to earn it. Good coaches make athletes pay the price.

Let's Have Some Fun

I can't count the number of times I said this to a team before taking the field for a game. It's one thing to pay the price by working hard and making personal sacrifices for the good of the team; it's quite another to have fun once in a while. Good coaches understand that youngsters must have both in relatively equal measure. I learned quite early, for example, never to take myself or my sport too seriously. I learned to poke fun at myself and to back away from constant hard work to make sure the kids laughed once in a while.

The Hard Battles Are the Most Satisfying

Good coaches understand that the purpose of practice and all the hard work it involves is to perfect the entire team in order to make winning easier. But, even given all that, good coaches and committed athletes don't get excited about easy victories. Sounds like a contradiction, doesn't it? But the fact is, committed coaches and athletes find their greatest satisfactions in the toughest contests, the hardest-fought victories. What we love is the pulse-pounding challenge of a worthy opponent. Only then can we discover new strengths within ourselves and find the satisfaction of a total commitment.

Kids Need Something to Get Excited About

If kids are unable to find something worthwhile to get excited about, they'll come up with something else—and their parents and coaches may not like it. Psychologist Henry

Murray indicated years ago that the natural curiosity of children and their need for sensory stimulation will often cause them to seek offbeat, even harmful experiences. Sports provides an outlet for this need for excitement. Good coaches use the inherent excitement of competition to get kids to commit to the kinds of activities that promote not only winning programs but the character development of their athletes.

Kids Need Someone to Respect

Athletes will commit to a sport they are lukewarm about if they like and respect the coach. As indicated in Chapter One, children actually need to identify and yield to a respected adult. Murray called this a need for deference. Whatever we call it, good coaches take advantage of it. But they also realize that to be respected, their commitment, self-denial, and courage must be evident in their own behavior. They know that the will to win and the self-discipline that accompanies it must be perfected in themselves before they can hope to perfect it in others.

HOW PARENTS TEACH COMMITMENT:

When You're Green, You Grow; When You're Ripe, You Rot

Kids must understand that they can always get better—at everything they do. And when the primary goal is to reach out to others, they learn the value of self-sacrifice and grow toward real commitment. They also learn that self-sacrifice is never completely unselfish; the giver always gets something in return. Let's admit it. The media populate our world with people who are beautiful, talented, fascinating, even brilliant—but rarely generous, more rarely completely unselfish.

Only unselfish people receive much in return. The satisfactions found in selflessness are priceless. The parent who teaches such lessons to her children provides them a sense of direction that leads only to happiness in life. It is a lesson that emphasizes "us" over "me" and self-sacrifice over self-indulgence. It involves giving more than you have and taking less than you want, and it proves that paying the price is more satisfying than footing the bill.

A friend of mine in Wisconsin is a member of the local Jaycees and spends time every November and December collecting and repairing old toys for distribution to needy families at Christmas. He suggested that his club gather donations to provide a turkey and a basket of food to the parents while giving the toys to the kids.

As his children got older, he brought each of them with him, first to paint toys, then to distribute them on Christmas Eve. At first reluctant to go with their dad to the collection center, the kids eventually started putting their coats on before being asked. They even started donating their own toys and sharing their allowances to buy food. And on Christmas Eve, when the children first experienced the toys and food being shared with the families, they stood transfixed in the snow, overwhelmed by the wonder of what they were doing.

Isn't This Fun?

Now that's fun! And what a remarkable standard for success. Here was a father who taught his children to measure themselves by the good they did, not by the "goods" they got. To him, as with most good coaches, fun was paying the price, and it involved much more than a self-centered romp through the local shopping mall. It involved cooperation, commitment to others, and personal sacrifice, and it led to a deep personal satisfaction far more profound than the short-lived pleasure of buying another pair of shoes.

Unlike all those youngsters abandoning their sports because they're not having any fun, these kids won't quit reaching out to others. Giving changes the lives of those we touch, and it changes ours. These kids lived Arthur Ashe's quote: "With what we get, we can make a living; with what we give, we can make a life."

To Appreciate It, Work for It!

A friend of mine used to tell her basketball team: "The harder you work, the harder it is to give up." The more an athlete gives in practice, the more she gets during the game. She also finds it harder and harder to stop trying. The initial investment of time and energy is too great. She's had to work too hard to give up now.

Good parents do the same thing with their children. The child who commits herself to homework every night will give a little more time and effort before the big test. The child who uses some or all of her allowance to buy designer jeans doesn't throw them on the floor and walk on them until mom rescues them for a good washing. Similarly, the child who pays for some or all of his college education is less likely to squander time and money in a succession of frat parties and barroom binges.

The harder we work, the harder it is to quit. And when we work for what we receive in life, we not only enjoy it more but we develop the character and emotional strength that derives from commitment. Parents who spoil their children with lots of gifts and little responsibility do them a disservice. They fail to recognize that when their children's ability to acquire material things outdistances their ability to enjoy them, they and their parents are in for a lot of trouble.

Get High on Life

The same is true of kids who find their excitement in drugs, sex, and violence. My friend's kids who stood in the snow that Christmas Eve to share toys and food with needy families experienced a real high. It involved a few moments of subdued excitement that exhilarated them and that probably lasted a lifetime. Children who miss out on life's natural highs get their kicks somewhere else, usually with pot or alcohol.

Another friend expects his kids to put some of their allowance into the collection plate every Sunday in church. He pads their allowances to make the gift a little easier, but they don't know that. At first, he almost had to pry the money from their clutching little fists, but, with time and persistence, they became eager to drop the money in the plate. My friend indicates that once they even high-fived each other when they gave a little more than usual.

There's nothing like the smile on a child's face when he puts money in a collection plate, repairs toys for the needy, or delivers a casserole to a sick neighbor. That's why it's a good idea to invite your children—even expect them—to join you when you do good. Thoughtfulness is contagious. It's one bug we want our kids to catch routinely. And, as indicated in Chapter One, there is no better way to connect with your kids.

Finding the Best Role Models

And is there a better way to earn your child's respect? As indicated often in this book, the best role models available to kids should be sitting at the dinner table with them. The good news is that children spend the better part of their lives *wanting* to respect and admire their parents. A child's need for deference is almost as powerful as his need for others to think well of him. Most powerful, however, is his need to think well of himself.

What Kids *Need* to Commit To

Youngsters must satisfy a variety of very important needs. They need to feel safe, to belong, to feel good about themselves, to accomplish, and to be recognized. They need to impress others, to help others, even to yield to others. These are their motivations. In essence, the desire to satisfy these needs causes them to behave in certain ways.

What a wonderful reality for you and me. These are the very things we *want* them to do. The key for us is to get them to satisfy these needs the right way and within the right context.

In order to do that, we need a framework within which to operate, and none is better than the framework provided by psychologist Abraham Maslow. A football coach joining forces with a renowned academic? You bet! Great coaches are master psychologists. I lay no claim to being a great coach, but I hope that I'm a better-than-average student of psychology. Maslow, especially, impressed me with the simplicity and the broad application of his theory. I've used it as a coach, a teacher, a counselor, an administrator, and a parent.

It consists of five levels of needs. The levels apply to all of us. Physiological needs are the lowest on Maslow's hierarchy. They are followed by safety needs, social needs, ego needs, and self-actualization needs. Important to Maslow's thinking is the idea that lower level needs must be satisfied before upper level needs become motivators.

In other words, kids won't worry about their safety if they're hungry. The physiological need for food must be satisfied before the child is motivated to be safe. That's why children in poverty will steal food in plain sight of store owners. Similarly, until the child feels safe, he or she won't care about belonging to a social group. If constantly threatened, for example, athletes are unable to become a team, and children are unable to become a family. Maslow suggests much more. I've always thought he would have been a marvelous coach. Here's why.

Physiological Needs

The first set of needs that Maslow identified are on the physiological level: hunger, thirst, warmth, shelter, etc. We may take for granted that these needs are being met for our own children, but they may not always be met for all the young people we or our teens come in contact with.

Take food, for example. Sometimes the problem is not having enough to eat, but of eating the right type of food. Without the right mixture, kids simply don't perform as well, and poor performance affects their level of commitment. Kids will operate at peak performance and make strong commitments with the right "fuel" mix, and they'll run out of gas when their diet consists mainly of fast foods and between-meal snacks.

Safety Needs
When physiological needs are satisfied, the child is motivated to be secure. He wants to feel safe. Good coaches understand that; when athletes seek safety, they'll listen to coaching pointers that prevent injury. They'll also look to coaches and teammates for a sense of security, both on the field and in the school and community. In this regard, teams are families; and, true to the old saying, families are the one place in our lives that have to take us in.

Good coaches know that the team as a family needs discipline to hold it together. But they also know that it takes more than that. Discipline, especially punitive discipline, often threatens kids. Good coaches and good parents promote self-discipline by preserving the family with love. Such love also creates commitment.

When the storm and strife of life in our changing world start to weigh on us, it's comforting to find a safe harbor. Such a harbor might involve relationships at football practice, the safety of a counselor's office, a mother's embrace, or the love of family. Certainly, it is all of these and more, but none is more important than the security of a loving home. Kids can tolerate a lot during the day, whether at school or in the community, as long as they know that home is more than a group of related strangers.

Like good coaches, parents realize that youngsters need to believe in something larger than themselves. They require a daily spirituality that puts their lives in perspective. They may not require denominational prayer in their schools, but they do need a deep spirituality that guides their behavior and gives them a sense of security, a spirituality that may include religion but that may go even further.

Such a spirituality discovers, embraces, and commits to causes that are larger than ourselves, whether those causes be God, family, country, or the humanity that daily surrounds us. The school and the family that secures itself in such spirituality helps children feel safe and gives youngsters purpose and a sense of direction. It is this spirituality, sorely missing in most of our nation's schools, that is needed to prevent more Columbines.

Social Needs

Once children feel loved and secure, they'll seek a sense of belonging, of "teamness," of social acceptance. Good coaches realize that until the physiological and safety needs of athletes are satisfied, kids are unable to become a team. Threatened and insecure athletes, like the rest of us, are too busy seeking escape from threat to feel any sense of belonging. So good coaches make kids feel secure by talking to them personally, getting to know them, thanking them for their contributions, and, yes, giving them a hug or a pat on the back every once in a while.

Once secure, however, they want to identify with a certain group. Once identified with it, they will become extraordinarily loyal—no matter what the group. Just say *Semper Fi* to a marine, then stand back and watch. Or threaten someone in front of his gang members. Or discriminate against a union member. Or challenge a New York firefighter in front of his or her brothers. Or seek to harm big brother's little sister. Other members of our group are very important to us because they help us understand who we are.

We all need to belong to something. We all need to be needed. We are social creatures, dependent on each other not just for survival but for self-awareness. This is especially true of youngsters, who find their self-identity reflected in the acceptance of parents and friends. If those two very disturbed young men at Columbine High School, for example, had felt accepted at school, they never would have sought personal affirmation in senseless violence.

Violence, not connectedness, was their path to recognition. If some kids are unable to find recognition the right way, they'll find it the wrong way. But they *will* find it, and they will also find acceptance. They may not be accepted on the football team or in the chess club, student government, or a loving family. Their acceptance may come from gangs or other student fringe groups that find recognition in theft, drugs, violence, and other anti-social behaviors.

Reflect on this for just a moment. Not only do these children learn to operate on the fringes of our society and engage in these kinds of activities, but they find their role models there. I recall years ago hearing a freshman girl shouting to her friends in the school cafeteria, "Devil Angel is coming next week! Devil Angel is coming!" I discovered later that Devil Angel was a gang leader, a recognized drug dealer, and an accused murderer.

This child, a student in our school for only two months and already a regular visitor to the Dean's Office, was absolutely rapturous at the thought of his visit. Maybe she had a tough home life or didn't have the ability to handle the academic and extracurricular expectations of her new school. Maybe she was frustrated and forced to share her personal identity with a drug-dealing murderer. If so, what an indictment of our schools for their exclusive preoccupation with academic and extracurricular "accomplishment."

Academics and extracurricular activities are fundamental within our nation's schools. But there is a growing number of people who seek additional ways for young people in our homes and schools to find recognition, success, and belonging. Many schools and homes across the country are engaging adolescents in volunteer activities that don't require academic or athletic skills, just a willingness to reach out to others and to perfect the sensitivity that makes them and others happy. When helping others is a standard for success, then accomplishment, recognition, and acceptance are within reach of every child. The home that promotes such a standard may still seek academic and extracurricular effort, but it also broadens each child's world by acknowledging the needs of others and by emphasizing the deep sense of personal satisfaction kids feel when they commit to helping others meet their needs.

Ego Needs

Kids can't be true to who they are until they *know* who they are, and they can't know who they are until they feel accepted by a group that's important to them. Good coaches understand that only through mutual caring and support can kids develop the personality and the ego strength that gives them the confidence to express their physical and emotional uniqueness, to develop self-control, and to make meaningful commitments. The satisfaction of ego needs gives athletes the strength and drive not only to establish lofty goals—but to accomplish them. Good coaches create such families and build, rather than battle, all those developing egos.

"Now that I'm fed, safe, and accepted, I can really start to discover who I am!" Only after children's fundamental needs have been satisfied does their need for self-discovery become a motivator. In other words, children have to be safe and accepted before they are able to develop a sense of self. Their need isn't simply to belong. It's to be understood and accepted—appreciated as individual and unique persons. It involves satisfying interactions and relationships with respected persons in their lives.

Such interactions and relationships provide the perceptions of others when we develop our own self-concepts. If parents call Tommy stupid, he'll think of himself as stupid. If parents tell him repeatedly how wonderful he is, he'll think of himself as wonderful. We condition our children's self-perceptions every day by how we interact with them. Not only does being accepted enable us to develop ego strengths, but it influences the kinds of ego strengths we develop.

Our culture's preoccupation with "things" is an obstacle for young people's ego development. It's intriguing how some teenagers who demand independence and individualism at every turn manage to dress in the same brand of jeans and wear the same hairstyles. Parents can't deny the influences of our social groups—on themselves as well as on their children. Just consider how we connect with "things" in our lives. I am my Harley; my Harley is me. I am my Lexus; my Lexus is me. Things can be extensions of our personalities, but they pale before the absolute influence of people we love and respect.

Let me introduce you to Rob. Rob was short, overweight, slow, and, in every sense of the word, a pacifist. He was everything a football player should *not* be. But his heart was as big as his X-large T-shirts, and his courage was evident every time he struggled to put his shoulder pads on. His coaches and teammates understood him. We understood that he loved football and simply wanted to be on the team.

We appreciated this, and we accepted him for his courage to try to play the game we all loved in spite of his obvious limitations. We all became teammates. He was no more or no less than anyone else on the team. He enjoyed being with us, and we enjoyed being with him. He liked that. He learned to live with his limitations because he thrived on the knowledge that we recognized and appreciated his courage and determination.

By contrast, consider what a lack of acceptance can do. Consider a young man I talked to a few years ago. Call him Jack. Jack acknowledged that he had been "on the fringes of his family" since he was a child. Subordinated to his brother, the favored child in the family, Jack and his sister never seemed to satisfy their mother. As a result, Jack was directionless for years, periodically getting into trouble as a teenager and, to this day, struggling to establish himself in a satisfying job.

Only with such understanding and acceptance can the Robs and Jacks of this world reach deep within themselves, discover who they are—and like what they find. Isn't that true of all of us? It's so much easier to love when you are loved, to discover who you are as reflected in the eyes of others, and to risk the search for the inner you because you know that others already like what you're about to find. Only at such moments are young people able to make commitments to be all they can be.

Self-Actualization Needs

To Maslow, self-actualization meant "to be all you can be." Isn't that the goal every parent seeks for kids? Accomplished athletes with a solid sense of self become the best they can be. At the beginning of each season, coaches find a mob of virtually untapped potential standing before them. Their job is to make something of it by getting kids to make something of themselves.

Coaches also understand that complete potential is nothing. Potential must be actualized to become something. Good coaches understand that the youngster who says, "I could have been a great softball player" is not a great softball player and probably never will be. Good coaches don't permit such silliness. They provide the security, the social acceptance, and the ego-building support that actualizes potential and that results in a total commitment from their athletes.

I taught Maslow's theory to graduate classes in a local university for twenty-three years, and it still amazes me to realize that only after all these needs have been satisfied can people make something of their potential. In essence, none of us will ever be what we are capable of being until our physiological needs are satisfied and we are safe, appreciated for ourselves, and accepting of who we are.

Once all these other needs have been satisfied, children are motivated to push themselves beyond perceived limits, to become all they are capable of becoming. Self-actualizing youngsters are able to make commitments because they believe in themselves and in others. They have the strength of character to assume significant responsibilities because they know they can handle them.

A friend of mine coaches football at Mt. Carmel High School in Chicago, my former high school. One of the finest football programs in the nation with a record nine state championships in Illinois, Mt. Carmel has winning traditions that date back to 1923. It is alive and well today because the kids feel safe with their coaches and teammates, belong to a winning program, and are proud of who they are. I felt the same way back in . . . well, never mind.

Their coach, Frank Lenti, reminds them of their commitment before every game. He gathers them around him just before leaving the locker room and shouts, "Who's responsible for this game?" They answer, "I am!" He shouts, "Who?" And they shout, even louder, "*I* am!" Then, he tells them to take the field and play football. Needless to say, they take the field with such purpose and commitment that their opponents spend more time watching them than getting ready for the game.

Responsibility can do that. Children who not only pay the price but accept responsibility learn to self-actualize. Ultimately, they make commitments and accomplish great things in life because they believe in themselves and behave accordingly. The Roman poet Virgil said, "They conquer who believe they can." Ben Franklin said, "Energy and persistence conquer all things." And Vince Lombardi said, "Keep going— keep going and you will win." From ancient poets to contemporary football coaches, commitment and persistence are the pathways to success. They also lead to character.

The Tyranny of Talent

Sometimes commitment and self-actualization can go too far. A child's talent in one area can consume everything else in his or her life. It can assume an existence of its own that demands expression. Such demands for kids, as with many adults, are virtually irresistible. At such times, kids need another kind of help. Let me borrow a couple paragraphs from an article I wrote for the *NCAA News* a few years ago:

> Some athletes possess a special athletic genius that can take control of their lives. From Van Gogh in painting and Mozart in music to Einstein in math and science, genius is so undeniable that it *demands* expression. Music echoed through Mozart's mind; he simply wrote it down. Completed paintings appeared in Van Gogh's mind; he simply put them on canvas. Einstein's mind worked until entire blackboards were filled with equations. And Michael Jordan found himself in "the zone," making a succession of three-point shots that even he couldn't understand.
>
> The point is, the undeniability of such genius can sublimate everything else in one's life. It can provoke an absence of self-discovery.
>
> Athletics is no different. The youngster who dribbles her way through a maze of defenders and "double pumps" a lay-up and the young halfback who litters the field with would-be tacklers create moments that mystify themselves as well as everyone in the stands. Their self-discovery affirms their athletic genius but provides few insights into who they are as persons.

When commitment and self-actualization go to this extreme, they leave room for little else in a child's life. Class work and relationships at home suffer; so do social relationships. At the extreme, such youngsters can become so spoiled, they ignore social protocols, rules, and even laws to satisfy their own needs. And this isn't restricted to just sports. Some kids are gifted in music or drama or with cars or computers. They devote time and energy every day to the activity for two reasons: they're good at it, and they feel good doing it.

Coaches and parents can't play into this trap. It restricts movement in other areas, and it causes isolation. And the biggest problem is that it defines success for the child within only one context. Whatever it is, it becomes the child's standard of success. When the child's feelings of self-worth are dependent on his success or failure in a single activity, for example, incompetence is guaranteed in almost every other area of the child's life.

Well, we know we don't want *that* for our kids. Even as a coach, in spite of my preoccupation with my sport, I knew that the development of my athletes as complete human beings was my utmost goal. Recognizing that they loved football because they were good at it and had fun doing it, I decided to use those same standards to introduce them to other aspects of their personalities. Parents can do the same thing. Consider the following suggestions.

Help Them Uncover Their Real Needs

Kids need recognition to develop and reinforce their self-worth. They want to *be* somebody, to make a difference, to be accepted, to satisfy, even exceed the expectations of important others in their lives. This need for recognition is complemented by other important needs in children's lives. Kids also need to accomplish something difficult, to overcome weakness, to be independent, to control others, and to be free to follow impulses.

When coaches and parents help kids acknowledge and satisfy these needs, they help them develop and refine the tools for achieving recognition. It is well known among psychologists and teachers that if a child's performance on a certain task is seen as a real measure of his worth as a human being, he will go to great lengths to perform well. Kids are no different from us in that regard. So the question is, what other tasks, besides those things he or she excels in, do we place before them as challenges?

Learn to Appreciate the Satisfaction of Those Needs

The more we as parents and coaches specifically recognize other kinds of successes, the more we provide opportunities for our teens to feel good about themselves. Good coaches understand that no matter how talented young athletes might be, their gifts are never proof of their worth as people. The media and an admiring public may reserve floors on Mt. Olympus for Wayne Gretzky, Michael Jordan, and several others, but, when all is said and done, they are not gods, just gifted athletes.

In fact, what really distinguishes them as media darlings is their ability to defy gravity—and one or two other natural laws—*and* to reject the me-first mindset and the simple-minded immaturity that characterizes so many other college and professional athletes.

Everything Can Come to a Crashing Halt!

Many years ago, I was the starting fullback at Marquette University when they decided to drop football. About a month into my second semester, I received an offer to play professional football for the Calgary Stampeders up in Canada. A few weeks later, I received a phone call from the Dallas Cowboys with another offer. I decided instead to transfer to the University of Nebraska to complete my senior year and to get my degree in education.

Just before my senior year at Nebraska, I was told by my coach that the Pittsburgh Steelers and a couple other football teams were interested in me. Two weeks into practice for that season, I incurred a cerebral hemorrhage and suddenly discovered that "Mike the football player" was gone. Any chance to play my senior year and to try my hand at the pros ended. And it all happened with one thump on the head that destroyed my vision for about thirty seconds.

Kids Must Look Beyond a Single Dream

Everything can come to a crashing halt just that quickly. Football players get cerebral hemorrhages and other career-ending injuries; pianists break fingers; painters lose their vision; rock guitarists break their wrists. Life can throw some terrible and shocking surprises our way, all the more terrible when we have nowhere else to turn when the shock is over. At such times, shock gives way to hopelessness and to major adjustments in our lives.

Such hopelessness can be avoided if coaches and parents help kids explore interests and activities *outside* the scope of their special talents. Frank Sinatra and Tony Bennett are also accomplished painters. Hall of Fame defensive tackle Rosey Grier loved needlepoint! Vince Lombardi wanted to be a priest. Jim Thorpe won essay and dancing contests. In between moments of running into my fellow man, I loved to write poetry. I was also fortunate to discover that, once my playing days were over, I also loved to teach it.

We Must Love Ourselves Before We Can Love Anyone Else

Exploring a range of interests and developing different aspects of our personalities is personally rewarding. We learn more about ourselves and we get to know ourselves better. Invariably, we find something we like. Liking ourselves is the ultimate goal, the single most important element in any child's journey toward self-discovery. Without self-love, we are incapable of loving others.

Children who fail to achieve self-love are unable to draw upon inner resources. They have none. They are unable to find inner strength during times of adversity. They have little. They are unable to look inside themselves to just feel good. There is little to feel good about. So, like all the rest of us, they look outside themselves—for things, for external affirmation. They want more and more from the outside because they find less and less on the inside.

An exclusive focus on one talent or interest creates one-dimensional kids, some of whom ultimately become unable to commit to anything else. They are too consumed by their talent.

Change the Anchor Point

Kids need our help to combat the demands their talent imposes on them. To do this successfully, coaches and parents must understand that the child's overcommitment to one activity represents an *anchor point* in his life. His commitment holds him in one place and prevents movement. To provoke change, we have to move his anchor point.

To accomplish this, we suggest closely related and some-what desirable alternatives to the current activity. We are careful not to make the alternative activities too extreme. The child might reject them immediately. The alternatives should be enjoyable and acceptable, perhaps related to the child's primary interest. The point is, by moving anchor points ever so slightly, we eventually promote meaningful change in the child's range of interests and activities.

Frequent interaction helps move anchor points. Consider one of the dialoguing techniques discussed earlier in this book, Reversing. It is used in the following sample dialogues.

Dialogue - Reversing

Consider this discussion between a coach and his gifted athlete after the last game of the season.

COACH TO PLAYER

Coach: Tommy, great season. You were as good a halfback as I've ever had, and you're not afraid of work. That combination makes for a great leader.

Player: Thanks, Coach. Now let's see if any colleges feel like you do.

Coach: College? You have your senior year to go first. And what about those grades? I see they dipped last quarter. (Identify the problem)

Player: No sweat. My ACT was 18, and I'm in the upper half of my class. The NCAA won't nail me.

Coach: What makes you think college coaches want guys who just get by? Learning all your offensive and defensive assignments and getting good grades in the classroom are just as important to them as your performance on the field. (Expand on the problem)

Player: Yeah? Good point. Well, I guess I could work harder.

Coach: Well, let's put it this way—what will happen if you don't? (Use reversing technique)

Player: I don't know; I guess I won't get better grades.

Coach: What could happen then? (Probe for deeper insights)

Player: Well, I guess I could slip into the lower half of my class.

Coach: Yeah, what else? (Seek additional insights)

Player: Some of the college coaches might not be interested in me?

Coach:	Right on target, kid. You tell me; is it worth it?
Player:	Probably not. OK, point made. I'll hit the books a little harder.
Coach:	Good idea. Weren't your English grades pretty good last year?
Player:	Yeah. I always kinda liked English, especially writing.
Coach:	I have an idea. Do you want to hear it? (Asking permission assures that the athlete continues to "own" any solutions)
Player:	Sure.
Coach:	Why don't you see Mr. Tomlinson to see if you can do some sports writing for the school newspaper. You could give some real behind-the-scenes looks at what goes on—not only here but with other sports. (Introduce a related activity to help move the athlete's anchor point)
Player:	Yeah, I guess I could do that. It might be fun to be the resident jock reporter.
Coach:	Good! Now how am I going to know you've done all this? (Assure some accountability)
Player:	I'll check in next week.
Coach:	How about Friday? There, it's on my calendar. See you then. (Assure specifics of accountability)

PARENT TO CHILD

Child:	Boy, we were rocking last night.
Parent:	Yes, I suspect you guys are getting pretty good. You certainly spend enough time together.
Child:	Lotsa practice, Mom. Gotta practice!
Parent:	Yes, I'm sure you do, but you sure don't see many of your other friends, and,

	frankly, I'd like to see you hit the books a little more. (Identify the problem)
Child:	Come on, Mom, you know we have to practice. It's paying off, too. My other friends know what I'm doing, and my grades aren't *that* bad.
Parent:	OK, then just for the sake of discussion, what could happen if you don't improve your grades or don't maintain contact with your old friends? (Use the reversing technique)
Child:	I have new friends in the band, and my grades are good enough, even to study music in college. And, hey, we could make a lot of money right now!
Parent:	Yes, that's a possibility, and my money's on you. I think you *should* be rewarded for all your hard work. But what will happen with the band if you don't handle that money correctly? (Use reversing technique again)
Child:	Hey, since when don't I know what to do with money?
Parent:	Well, I've never seen you do much with the taxes and the family budget.
Child:	Taxes?
Parent:	Yes, just ask your dad about them. Until you find a way to own your own country, you're going to have to pay taxes when you earn money. Who manages your band? Who will handle the travel budget, equipment replacement, and all that other good stuff? (Expand on the problem)
Child:	I don't know; we never thought of that.
Parent:	Well, I have an idea. Do you want to hear it? (Asking permission assures that the child continues to "own" any solutions)

Child: Yeah, sure.

Parent: What about contacting your counselor to see about some business classes next semester? Your band could be your project, and aren't several of your old friends in some of those classes? They could help you. (Introduce a related activity to move the child's anchor point, a related activity that could introduce him to bookkeeping, accounting, and more math—and reunite him with a few old friends)

Child: You know—that's not a bad idea. Maybe I'll check her out tomorrow.

Parent: Great, and I'm sure you know that math will help and so will English with the letters you'll have to write.

Child: OK, Mom, don't knock me out with all these wonderful ideas of yours!

Parent: OK, OK, I'll hold off on those. But let me know what happens with your counselor. Maybe we can talk about what she says at dinner. (Maintain some accountability)

Let's Wrap It Up

Commitments are much more than decisions, even promises. They are covenants, solemn and binding pledges between two or more people. When children make such commitments, they must be expected to honor them. Sometimes, they'll forget them. After all, a commitment may be the perfect example of something that's easier said than done. So our job is to hold their feet to the fire, not to hurt them, just to get their attention. Kids have to be accountable for their pledges as well as their behavior. That's why any commitment must come from the child. Parents may influence it, even help shape it, but a commitment made at the request of Mom or Dad is soon forgotten when Mom and Dad are gone. Coaches and parents must be role models. They must behave in ways that encourage commitments from kids, not speak in ways that demand them.

Consider once again this issue of role models. Never was the issue clearer than when terrorists destroyed the World Trade Center. The entire nation learned by watching the NYC fire and police departments and the volunteer workers that role models are much more than pro basketball's high-flying slamma-jammars. We learned that legitimate role models shock us, not with their bizarre behavior, but with their selfless commitment to causes that are larger than themselves.

By observing the dedication and courage of such role models, we actually want to be better people. That's what good role models do. They don't just model occupationally limiting skills like stuffing a basketball. They model the kinds of skills that make us feel good about ourselves. Their examples are so pure and so unencumbered by their own vested interests that they are morally and spiritually inspirational. We must *be* such role models for our children. "OK, wait a minute," you say. "You want me to go through life with my kids being morally and spiritually *inspirational?*"

Yes. If *we* don't live the virtues and the values we expect of our kids, we can never expect to see them reflected in *their* behavior. Our influence with our children is far more profound than any of us realizes. Two of my grown-up daughters, Peggy and Carrie, were enjoying one of their now legendary two-hour phone conversations the other day. Peggy coaches a high school volleyball team in Chicago. Halfway through her comments about how she planned to discipline a couple of kids, Carrie, who now lives in Brooklyn, interrupted, "OK, *Dad*—wow, you sound just like Dad!"

Scary, isn't it? What a responsibility—but we're stuck with it. I only hope my youngest was talking about one of my better ideas. Like everyone else, I've had my share of duds. More to the point, I hope she lives by it and applies it consistently to everything she does, not just her coaching. Consistency and commitment go hand in hand. That's why consistency is the subject of the next chapter.

4

CONSISTENCY
Keeping an Eye on the Target

She was only 4'8" and weighed barely 85 pounds. More noticeable than her diminutive size were her freckles and a shock of flaxen hair as stubbornly resistant to a brush as Rachel was to believing she was too small to play basketball. Needless to say, Rachel was the shortest girl on the basketball court when the freshmen lined up for tryouts.

Her coach, Mrs. Dietrich, remembers her well. She remembers regarding Rachel as just another athletic wannabe. She remembers the shortest girl in school standing in line with the rest of the girls, her jersey almost falling off her shoulders and the hem of her shorts well below her knees. But mostly, she remembers Rachel's extraordinary energy. Rachel could galvanize the entire gymnasium with her attitude and enthusiasm. In fact, her desire won her a spot on the freshman B team.

A notch below the freshman A team, the B team allowed less gifted girls to be involved in the school's athletic program. And Mrs. Dietrich was careful to give every girl on the team an equal opportunity to play in each game. She knew that consistent effort often transformed seemingly limited athletes as freshmen into varsity starters as juniors and seniors. She also discovered that every time she fanned a flame like Rachel's, sparks would ignite everywhere in the gymnasium.

Athletes like Rachel were gifts to Mrs. Dietrich. Rachel rarely needed encouragement, in spite of her limitations. She constantly battled the disbelief of others as well as her own self-doubt. She overcame her own exhaustion when competing with the bigger and more talented girls. She never quit. It was as if her lack of size and talent created a consistency of effort and a depth of character that was somehow denied to other kids.

When her freshman season ended, Rachel committed herself to an off-season of conditioning and practice. She worked tirelessly, every day, forcing herself into the gym in spite of sore muscles and occasional self-doubts. She read sports biographies, studied basketball strategy, bought drill books, and watched basketball on TV.

Still only 4′10″ as a sophomore, Rachel tried out for the JV team. She made the team but played very little. Her junior year was much the same, but her senior year was different. She grew five inches over the summer and already was the best dribbler and one of the quickest players in the school. Rachel became the starting point guard on the varsity.

She set school records for assists and even accepted an offer to play for a small Division III school in a neighboring state. During the basketball season, whenever she could get home, she always visited Mrs. Dietrich. She usually made a point of talking to the freshman B team, sharing her experiences and the philosophy she learned from Mrs. Dietrich: "Make a consistent effort and think good thoughts, and you'll always be a winner—even if you lose once in a while."

What Is Consistency?

Consistency is standing tall no matter what life throws at us. It's smiling when things are tough, gritting our teeth and hitching up our belts when more work needs to be done. It's staying true to our values when temptation tries to nudge us in the wrong direction. Good parents and successful coaches understand that kids may lose once in a while but that they won't fail if they never quit. The willingness to persist, to work consistently toward our goals is itself a victory. For athletes and non-athletes alike, such character requires training, motivation, discipline, and conditioning. Coaches understand that such consistent traits must be drilled into their athletes.

Vince Lombardi once said: "Winning isn't everything. The *will* to win is everything. It is more important than any event that occasions it." To Lombardi, the outcome of the game was secondary to the consistent effort each player must make to win it. He realized that athletes who refuse to quit will win their share of games. Like most good parents, he also knew that they will develop the strength of character and the unconquerable spirit that result in a consistent "refusal to lose" in all walks of life. Coaches and parents understand that this is especially important in those areas that give us a sense of pride and self-worth.

Former heavyweight champ Jack Dempsey was asked once for his definition of a champion. He thought for a moment and answered, "A champion is someone who gets up—when he can't." What a remarkable quality, getting up when you can't. Don't we all as parents want this quality in our children—for that matter, in ourselves?

Nothing piques our sensitivities or our admiration more than the sight of someone struggling back to his or her feet after getting knocked down. The superstar who achieves effortlessly is a marvel; the fifth-stringer who refuses to stay down is an inspiration. He is an inspiration who understands that it's not the number of times you get knocked down that counts; it's the number of times you get up. We want our children to be inspirations. To us, they're already superstars.

The Power of Tradition

To develop the trait of consistency in our children, we must determine what is good and desirable in our families and then promote a focus on it until it becomes routine for everyone in the family. That's why tradition is best defined as "how we do business around here." Whether it's working hard or being considerate of other people, it's simply "what we do."

It takes a whole lot of time and a great deal of inspiration to make even the smallest tradition. But how quickly it grows when everything good in us is there to encourage it. And how quickly it rewards us. We give traditions love and reverence, and they give us strength. They bolster our belief systems and provide permanence in our lives. This is true not only of athletic teams but of every family in this country.

Consistency is a matter of good habits, and nothing promotes good habits better than the enduring example of tradition. Consider a few illustrations.

Building a Tradition

Notre Dame did it. You may love the school, or you may hate it, but you have to admit that it enjoys a storied name among the nation's universities. George Kelly, my former football coach at Marquette University and, later, at Nebraska, is a coaching fixture there, and he's the first to admit that the legend of Notre Dame results from the dedication and commitment of thousands of people. The two letters—ND—symbolize all those people and everything they did to establish the Notre Dame tradition.

The football team is reminded of that tradition every time they leave the locker room to take the field for a game. Just to the right of the exit door is a large "ND" painted about seven feet up the wall. After each player descends the flight of stairs approaching the exit, he touches the symbol with the fingers of his right hand. The gesture expresses his acknowledgment of the ND tradition as well as his commitment to everything the tradition represents.

Decades of adversities overcome and hard-fought victories are recaptured in one simple gesture. Tradition does not mean that the past is dead but that it lives on in the hearts and minds of new generations. That's why we want tradition to be on our side. It embodies everything that is important to us, and it exerts continuing influence on our youngsters. Highly visible symbols of such traditions are valuable reminders to youngsters that they are members of a special family and that certain responsibilities go with that membership.

Celebrating Our Identity

"I am who I am, and I'm proud of it." This should be the mantra of every young person in this country. Traditions that promote self-awareness and self-confidence in our children are ultimately more satisfying than forays into the local shopping mall and more enduring than a last-second plunge into the end zone for the winning score.

Kids won't do something special until they *are* something special. That we remind them of their uniqueness, their capabilities, and our expectations is one of our most important responsibilities as adults. Tradition can help us. Consider how it helps Mt. Carmel High School.

Getting Pride to Work for You

The Mt. Carmel football team has won more state championships than any other team in Illinois. They *expect* to win. They can honestly say, "We are who we are, and we're proud of it." In fact, they say it after every away game—on their way back to school in the bus. Just as they turn off Stony Island onto 64th Street, one of the captains in the bus shouts, "Get 'em up!" At the command, every player holds his helmet high above his head and chants the school fight song. They don't sing it; it's more a deep-voiced incantation, recited in unison. They refer to themselves in the song as "Carmel men," and they act the part. They are well-disciplined, responsible, and dedicated young men, members of Illinois' most consistently winning football team, enjoying and contributing to a tradition that grows each year.

Predictability Is Good

As parents and coaches, we all know that routines can have all the charm and excitement of leg irons, but they can also make a sometimes distracting world comfortably predictable. They can also keep kids doing what we want them to do. Good rituals and traditions are like habits, at first too weak to be felt and, later, too strong to be broken.

In sports, traditions take a long time to establish. They can be ruined in a few short years if current players choose to ride on the coattails of everyone who preceded them. The coach's job is to keep the tradition alive. Good coaches remind their players that winning traditions are like muscles. Either you work to keep them strong, or they go soft.

What's in a Name?

Well, contrary to Shakespeare's notions about roses, there's a lot in a name. Names are symbolic of some of the finest family traditions. You may not have an ND painted on the wall near your front door, but you have a family name that boasts its own intriguing traditions. Provide reminders of that tradition to serve as a continuing source of pride to kids in the family.

If you don't have a coat of arms, make one. Have the kids help make it by identifying the events, people, and concepts that are most important to the family. Make the design and display it prominently in the house. This may sound silly, but it works, especially if the kids have a chance to have input into its design.

This Is Who I Am

Another good idea is to display photographs of family members on one wall in the house. Especially important are pictures of grandparents, great-grandparents, and great-great grandparents. A wall full of such photographs reminds each child in the family that "this is who I am" and that "I am a part of something that is larger than myself." Identifying with something larger than ourselves, whether it's God, country, team, or family, relieves us of what can sometimes be a tiresome and unfulfilling focus on ourselves.

As William James said, "The great use of life is to spend it for something that will outlast us." Parents who spend their lives on their children understand this, and good family traditions provide such opportunities for children. Children learn that the people and causes outside themselves have great importance. They learn that the only way to get love is by loving, to make friends is by being one, and to find personal satisfaction is by seeking the satisfaction of others. Athletes learn to motivate themselves before a contest by motivating everyone else on the team, and children satisfy the search for themselves by discovering the worth of everyone around them.

The Reality of the Self-Fulfilling Prophecy

Children who are told consistently how loved and sensitive and good they are can't help but become loved, sensitive, and good. They'll even become smarter because they'll begin to believe in their abilities and to develop the consistency of effort that accompanies confidence.

Consider the story of the little engine. Starting his climb up the hill, he said, "I think I can; I think I can." Consistent effort almost always pays off.

Sometimes that support comes in the form of clear and reasonable expectations. Let's admit it; only the most devout little egghead relishes the idea of doing homework every night. But, like the pre-competition routine for athletes, an after-school or after-dinner routine for children gets homework and chores done, especially when the kids help plan it. If children help develop the routine, they feel a sense of control and will tend to commit more readily to the time it takes to complete important assignments.

Family Traditions

Celebrations of special occasions are among the family's most enduring traditions. Family get-togethers at Christmas, Passover, Thanksgiving, and birthdays provide some of the family's dearest and most lasting memories. Nothing sustains tradition or brings more happiness than warm memories. Memory provides lilacs and freshly mown grass in the dead of winter, and it revives the love of a deceased parent, other loved ones, and friends.

It's the Little Things That Count

Consider traditions like holding hands during a pre-meal prayer, reading to children after dinner, or singing to children at bedtime. My wife lost her father several years ago, but one of the fondest memories of her childhood is having him sing to her at bedtime. Her dad was the first to admit that he had a lousy voice, but that didn't make any difference to him or to her. Maybe love is even more genuine when people have the courage to express it out of tune.

Such memories and traditions provide a reminder of the value of family and promote a consistency of behavior in children that helps sustain the traditions and that gives the kids a sense of who they are. Constancy and permanence promote character development. Love can do that. It is the world's most powerful energy, and, like all energy, it never weakens or disappears. My wife still feels her father's love. I do, too. It's real.

Keeping Your Eye on the Target

The right direction is very important. Author Washington Irving once said, "Great minds have purposes; others have wishes." Purposes are targets for action; wishes are excuses for inaction. Kids need the kinds of realistic and worthwhile goals that promote consistent effort. We must remember that a young person's goals follow closely his or her needs.

So we must work closely with our adolescents to identify their most important needs. Remember that the child's goals must satisfy the child's needs, not the parents'. We want certain things for our kids that relate to *our* goals. The child's goals will relate to his or her needs.

It's important, then, to discuss needs and to develop goals with kids. Adolescents can learn several important lessons from this goal setting, including:

* that goals promote a consistency of purpose as well as the consistent effort to realize them;
* that sometimes we need help identifying our most important goals;
* not to disown a goal just because someone else might sneer at it;
* not every need must be indulged—some, like the need for sex and excitement, must at times be denied;
* that it is one thing to recognize that a goal can't be satisfied, and quite another to convince yourself that the need behind it doesn't exist.

Good coaches recognize that goals provide a sense of purpose, they encourage a focus on important activities, and they promote the consistency of effort that leads to success. Coaches encourage goals that are SMART: Specific, Measurable, Adjustable, Realizable, and Time-Oriented.

Athletic goals may not have these components at all times, but they always focus on the achievement of a specific standard. Track coaches don't tell high jumpers to simply jump higher; they tell them to increase their vertical jump by three inches within a six-week period of time.

The point is, good coaches recognize that performance and process are much more important than outcome. They understand that if the athlete's performance improves, the outcome will improve. If the entire volleyball team improves its skills (performance), they will win more games (outcome). Performance goals change behavior. Consider the following examples.

HOW COACHES TEACH CONSISTENCY:

Specify, Specify, Specify

Good coaches understand that telling athletes to "Try harder" and "Do better" rarely gets the job done. The kids may respond by trying harder and struggling to do better, but if no one tells them *how* to do better, their performance doesn't change. The smart football coach doesn't say, "Try harder to pass block next year." He says, "I want you bench pressing 250 pounds by next season so your punch and lift improve, and I want to see a wider base and better bend in your knees every time you pass block!"

Measure, Measure, Measure

Similarly, the smart basketball coach doesn't say, "I want you to get more rebounds." She says, "I want your vertical jump to increase by four inches by next year." Or the track coach says, "I want you to squat 350 pounds by next season; I want a ten percent increase in your hamstring flexibility; and I want two-tenths of a second off your 100 meter time."

Adjust as Needed

Kids must help develop goals. If the coach sets the goal, the coach owns it. If the athlete helps set the goal, the athlete owns it. I always wanted my athletes to own their goals. I also realized that kids will sometimes set goals that are unrealistic or that, for other reasons, need adjustment. For example, athletes need to set both long-range and short-range goals. For the young ice skater, the goal may be to earn her way into the top twenty skaters in her age group within the next three years. A shorter-range goal might be to qualify for at least two major competitions next year, and an even shorter-range goal might be to execute a double toe loop ninety percent of the time.

If she is unable to perfect the double toe loop, she may have to adjust her long-range goals. Or if, like most kids, her sights are set a bit too high, she might have to adjust her standards to correspond more closely to her abilities. This aspect of goal setting can be very touchy, so this section includes a sample dialoguing technique on Setting Goals.

Get Real!

Goals must be realizable. If the bar is set so high that the athlete never clears it, he'll stop trying. That's another reason why performance or process goals are so important. A competition with myself is a competition I can win. I can always improve a little. On the other hand, if I say I will win every contest this year, to lose just one might hit me so hard that I stop trying to win the rest.

Outcome goals should result from process or performance goals. If I improve my performance, I probably will win more often. The key for good coaches, then, is to emphasize effort and performance over winning. Let the winning take care of itself. Athletes and coaches must learn to control what they can control—namely, the effort that goes into the contest and the practice that leads up to it.

Time Is Always a Factor

Establishing a goal within a specific time period can be enormously motivating to an athlete, especially if the youngster helps develop the goal. If the athlete is genuinely invested in the goal, corrective feedback within the time period is also motivating. If, for example, I've been slicing my drive into the woods for the first four holes, I want some advice to correct my problem before I finish the first nine holes. I have a goal, and I'm motivated to reach it. All I want are a few good suggestions.

Evaluation is most effective when kids want it. Evaluation is valuable when it helps young athletes realize their goals. It is less useful, even harmful, when they don't ask for it.

Goals Must Be Positive

Requested evaluation is motivating and positive; intrusive evaluation is negative. Be careful with it. When good coaches help athletes develop goals, therefore, they state them as positively as possible. The basketball coach helps her point guard increase her number of assists rather than decrease her number of bad passes. This way, young athletes focus on success rather than failure.

HOW PARENTS TEACH CONSISTENCY:

Let's Be Specific

Like a coach, a parent has to work alongside a child to set specific goals. Goals do little to improve behavior if kids have nothing specific to shoot for. Consistent effort requires a clear and desirable target. "Let's get that grade up in English" or "I want you to try a little harder around the house" are targets that are virtually invisible to kids. Sharpen the focus by helping the child learn how to read Shakespeare, understand the use of transposed appositives, or identify specific and routine tasks to be done around the house.

Make Sure We Measure Up

Introduce some measurement to the goals, and they become even clearer to kids. Children can learn how to read Shakespeare by reading along while they listen to audio tapes. They can understand transposed appositives by rereading that section of the textbook and by writing and sharing at least five examples. And they identify the time and manner of completing their chores around the house. Give them a great deal of input into such decisions. Remember, we're talking about *their* goals.

Nothing Is Etched in Stone

If Tom discovers halfway through the first tape that he still can't understand Shakespeare, have him tell you. He may want to persist a while longer, but if the strategy seems to be a flop, it's probably time to try something new. Flexibility is the key. You might want to read aloud and have him follow along. Or you might take one character, have him take another, and act out the play together.

If school or after-school responsibilities are piling up, it might also be wise to adjust the chores around the house, at least to adjust the time and manner of completing them. Adjusting a goal at the right time sustains its importance. Unrealizable goals, like unenforceable laws, lose their impact and become meaningless. Change them at the right time, and they'll keep working.

Give Them a Fighting Chance

The child who has a fighting chance to realize a goal will work at it. If Tom doesn't understand the fundamentals of a simple sentence, he'll throw up his hands at transposed appos101itives. If he sprained his wrist at wrestling practice, don't expect him to lift garbage cans. And if he's still reading at a sixth-grade level, Shakespeare will be about as clear to him as Einstein is to the rest of us. As with athletes, performance goals are the key. If Tom improves his skills with simple sentences and gets help with his reading, his grades (the outcome) will improve.

Winning in the classroom is just like winning in the stadium or the gymnasium. It can assume an importance all its own. When it's more important than effort, most kids will do anything to win. They'll cut corners and they'll cheat. Get them to put forth the right effort in relation to the right goals, and the grades will take care of themselves. So will their character. The grade is *not* the focus. What is most important is the effort to get it. I've worked with a lot of straight-A students who don't have a lot of *real* class.

Time Is My Friend

People who help me do my best are my friends. They might have to push pretty hard, but, sooner or later, they'll earn my respect. Time can provide such a push. Specific goals are excellent targets for action, but they become powerful incentives when deadlines are attached. Too much stress is bad; just the right amount gets us moving. When kids feel a little stress because of a deadline, they tend to work a little harder and a little faster.

If Tom develops the goal to get the garbage out by the curb right after dinner, he may need an occasional reminder, but he'll be more likely to do it. Specificity, measurement, and deadlines—essential elements in good goals.

* * * * * * *

A long-time friend indicates that she keeps three questions in mind when she helps her kids develop goals: "Specifically what do you plan to do?" "By when do you plan to do it?" And "How will I know you've done it?" The questions help her kids develop their own goals, include the specifics of what and when, and maintain the accountability we all need to stay on target. Following are some sample dialogues that can also help.

Dialogue - Setting Goals

COACH TO PLAYER

Player:	Well, this year's gotta be big for me.
Coach:	Don't worry about big years or little years, Kathleen. Just keep doing your thing and work to get better and better. (Suggest the need to look at performance goals) You've been a great player.
Player:	Yeah, but I have to improve in a couple areas. I know that.
Coach:	Good! I like the word "improvement"! It always signals good things. In what areas do you think you should improve? (Promote the player's self-evaluation)
Player:	Well, for one thing, I should be getting more rebounds.
Coach:	Yeah, more rebounds from you would help a lot. Anything else? (Probe for more self-evaluation)
Player:	More assists wouldn't hurt.
Coach:	OK, more assists. Can I toss in an idea or two? (Get permission to provide input)
Player:	I was counting on it!
Coach:	Well, you have a great shot inside the paint. Your percentage is good. What happens if one of your goals is to shoot more inside the paint?
Player:	More shots!? Now there's a goal I can live with!
Coach:	OK, now that I've made you so happy, let's talk specifics. What numbers are we looking at? (Push for specifics)
Player:	What do you mean?
Coach:	How many more rebounds per game, how many more assists, and how many more shots in the paint?
Player:	How about eight more rebounds and five more assists?

Coach:	Can you guarantee it? (Emphasize the realizability of the goals) Or do you want to gun for a number you are sure of?
Player:	Yeah, let's be sure of it. How about three or four more rebounds and two or three assists?
Coach:	Sounds good; let's go for three of each. And how about five more shots per game in the paint?
Player:	Well—if you insist!
Coach:	OK, kid, the numbers are right here in black and white. Let's go for it. (Document goals for future use)

PARENT TO CHILD

Child:	No way! Get me out of that class! I'll never pass it.
Parent:	Your math class? Why? What's the problem? (Ignore the comment about getting out of the class)
Child:	Old Jonesy hit us with two pop quizzes already, and I blew both of 'em.
Parent:	*Mr.* Jones surprised your class with two quizzes?
Child:	You got it! And I went down in flames both times.
Parent:	Well, what do you plan to do about it? (Use pushing technique)
Child:	Well, I guess you're going to have to get me out of there.
Parent:	Sorry, that's not an option. All your tests indicate that you have good ability, and I've become pretty well convinced that you're good in math. (Use boosting technique to re-establish the proper tone and go back to pushing technique) So where does that leave you?
Child:	Up the creek.

Parent:	OK, how are you going to get back down where the rest of us are? (More pushing technique)
Child:	Well, I gotta get better grades.
Parent:	What do you mean specifically? (Push for specifics)
Child:	I better get As on the rest of the quizzes.
Parent:	Can that be a sure thing? (Emphasize the realizability of the goal) Do you want to aim for something you're positive you can do?
Child:	I can get As if I want to!
Parent:	I'm with you! Remember me—the mom who believes in you? (More boosting technique) But you have other classes. What are you absolutely certain of?
Child:	I'll get Bs on the next three quizzes. If they're As, they'll be gravy. Then we'll talk—OK?
Parent:	Sounds great! I've got it: Bs on the next three quizzes. (Document the number) My money's on you.

Goals Lead to Solutions

Little has been said so far about *how* these goals will be realized. Goal setting determines *what* will be done—not *how* it will be done. Goals resolve problems, and the best definition of a problem is "a measurable or observable discrepancy between 'What is' and 'What should be'." It's the best definition I've ever heard. And it focuses on "what"—what is happening now and what *should* be happening in the future.

When the "what" has been determined and the goals have been developed and documented, it's time for "how"—*how* are we going to reach the goal(s)? That's the time for solutions, and any discussion of solutions with kids takes some skill, especially if you want them to have a hand in making the decisions. Getting kids to think for themselves involves some important techniques. Notice how the following sample dialogues use four effective techniques. Each of these techniques will be used repeatedly throughout the rest of the book:

- Probing: Helping the child look deeper into the issue.
- Elaborating: Getting the child to expand on the issue.
- Brainstorming: Helping the child explore alternative ways to reach goal(s).
- Clarifying: Helping the child look more clearly at the issue, avoid confusion, and improve focus.

Dialogue - Questioning Techniques

COACH TO PLAYER

Coach:	OK! Now that we have the numbers, *how* are we going to reach them?
Player:	What do you mean?
Coach:	How are we going to improve your rebounding, assists, and shots in the paint? (Clarifying technique)
Player:	I'll just work harder to get more rebounds and assists.
Coach:	Sounds good, but *how* are you going to work harder? What are some things you can do? (Brainstorming technique)
Player:	What about some drills?
Coach:	OK, talk to me about drills. How will drills help you reach your goals? What do you have in mind? (Elaborating technique)
Player:	For openers, I know that I have to work on my rebounding technique. I see on the game tapes that I'm still a little flat-footed sometimes.
Coach:	Why do you suppose that is? Can you think of some reasons? (Probing technique)
Player:	Dumb! Lousy habit. It's one I'd better break.
Coach:	Don't be so tough on yourself! You also happen to be a lot taller than most of your opponents. But that also might suggest a problem or two. Can you think of any? (More probing)
Player:	Yeah, I already know. I'm not boxing out the way I should.
Coach:	Way to go, kid. Nothing like some solid self-evaluation. It sounds as if you have a few things to work on. OK, let's talk about some drills. . . .

PARENT TO CHILD

Parent:	Whoops! Slow down, my friend; we're not done yet. First, let me congratulate you on the way you handled this whole thing. I think you did a nice job setting your goals.
Child:	Well, you know me, Mom. When you got it, you got it, and I am right up there. . . .
Parent:	Yeah, yeah, I know. It's wonderful being the mother of Mr. Terrific, but I have a question for you.
Child:	Shoot.
Parent:	Just *how* are you going to get those Bs?
Child:	No brainer! I'll just work harder.
Parent:	OK, talk to me about "work harder." Expand on that a little bit for me. (Elaboration technique)
Child:	Well, I'll spend more time each night on math, so Jonesy won't catch me napping.
Parent:	"More time." Specifically, what will you be doing during this time? What are some things that might make it quality time? (Brainstorming technique)
Child:	I guess I can review my notes. I can ask my math genius mom for help when I hit a snag. I can do some of the practice activities.
Parent:	And when are these really good ideas going to be done?
Child:	I'll find the time.
Parent:	Time seems to be an issue, doesn't it? It always is, I guess. How are you going to find this time? (Probing technique)
Child:	I usually have time after dinner, like at 7:00.
Parent:	Sounds good to me, if you're satisfied with it. . . .

Now, it's just a matter of keeping the youngster's feet to the fire. If your son is going to work on his math right after dinner, excuse him from the table after his fifth helping and send him on his way. It's one thing to set goals and find solutions; it's another to work toward them consistently. Consistency is the key to continued top-notch performance.

Pushing for Peak Performance

Recent research indicates that peak performance is similar in all athletes. Thousands of athletes indicated that when they were performing at their best, they were:

- *Self-confident*—They felt competent. They expected success. They didn't question themselves.
- *Focused*—They were not distracted. They focused completely on their performance. They were "in the flow," performing as if within a piece of music, lost in its rhythms and melody.
- *Effortless*—They weren't pressing or pushing themselves. They didn't tighten up by trying too hard.
- *Thinking positively*—They weren't thinking of failure. They expected only success. When they made a mistake, they learned from it but forgot it quickly and refocused on their performance.
- *Concentrating on process rather than outcome*—They thought only about the performance of their skills and didn't worry about winning or losing.

The manner in which coaches create the confidence, the focus, the positive thought, and the relative disregard for winning or losing is critical in the lives of athletes. The experiences coaches provide in relation to these characteristics often spell the difference between success or failure for athletes because they help establish the character athletes require to keep working hard at their goals.

Parents want to apply the principles exactly the same way. They want their children to perform at their absolute best, no matter what they're doing. Whether confronted with a final exam or the temptation to smoke pot, kids have to be at their best. Encouraging peak performances with children as with athletes, therefore, involves giving them confidence, encouraging focus, keeping their motivation at reasonable levels, thinking positively, and defining success as a function of effort, not just of achieving.

Competent and Confident

Competent athletes are self-motivated and consistent. So are competent kids. They're unafraid of hard work because they know it pays off. But how do we, as coaches and parents, make our young people competent? What principles can guide us? Well, we all know the answer to "How do you get to Carnegie Hall?"—"Practice, practice, practice." Practicing fundamental skills is the single most important thing we can teach our young people.

The mastery of fundamental skills determines the athlete's behavior during competition. Practice incorporates skillful performance into his or her body memory and creates an almost intuitive reaction to contest conditions. Skilled athletes don't think about their performance. In fact, thought slows down their reaction time. They simply react because they've been conditioned to react that way.

They react spontaneously, without hesitation. They react confidently and consistently because they know that they have developed the competence to perform skillfully. Very little distracts or upsets them. Competence, therefore, the kind that is conditioned into athletes, leads to self-confidence, which, in turn, leads to peak performance. Such competence also enables athletes to slow down time.

Parents who want their kids to be competent and confident recognize the need to build up rather than tear down. Give them confidence, a sense of control, and, like athletes, a mastery of the fundamentals. Once again the key is "Practice, practice, practice." As it does with athletes, practice determines behavior with children. Let's be honest, some parents do it better than others.

More than a few kids are "projects." We have all bumped into a project or two, the kind of child who needs almost constant attention and who leaves us slack-jawed even after our best efforts. Well, I submit that all kids are projects. They all should be wearing T-shirts that say, "Under Construction." Being construction projects, they require a solid foundation, careful planning, lots of attention, and constant reinforcement.

Stay on Task

When John Wooden conditioned his basketball players to disregard everything else when they set foot on the court, he was teaching them *focus*. When Phil Jackson emphasized Zen Buddhism with the Chicago Bulls and the Los Angeles Lakers, he was teaching them to live in the moment, not to be distracted by anything else—not the crowd, not the opponent, not a problem at home, not even their own intensity. Zen taught them *focus*.

Teens may not need Phil Jackson's emphasis on Zen, but they all have to learn to concentrate on the task at hand. When Tommy doesn't get the part in the play he wants, he can't allow his disappointment or possible embarrassment to interfere with an upcoming term paper. Nor can he allow his anger to spill over into his relationship with Maria. Maria will then have to be careful of the same thing. She may also get angry and break up with him, but she can't allow her emotions to disrupt her study routine.

Adolescents, like most adults, have to learn to put isolated moments of disappointment, even of tragedy, into separate boxes to be dealt with at the appropriate time. Whenever we are overwhelmed, whenever we feel trapped in a whirlpool of mounting responsibility, we become confused. The world seems to be moving too fast, so quickly that we feel unable to get ahold of even one event in our lives. The confusion that results seems to immobilize us. We have *so much* to do, we can't seem to find the time or the energy to do even one thing.

When confusion persists, peak performance is impossible. The key, as with good athletes, is to slow down time. Consider this example. Dinner is over and it's time for Tom to do his homework. Subtle hints don't work, not even Mom's patented "Look." It's time to delve into Tom's problem. In his room, you discover five books sitting on his desk, each requiring at least a half-hour of work. Tom simply doesn't know where to start; he feels immobilized.

Part of the solution? Remove four of the books so that Tom can't see them. Place one squarely in the center of the desk, and tell him to focus only on that assignment. Sound too simple? Maybe, but it works. Once he learns to focus on one thing at a time and to concentrate his energies, he discovers that he's able to get more done. He also discovers new levels of competence. Most important, he overcomes his confusion and impulse to do nothing.

The act of "slowing down time" may still sound scientifically impossible to you. If it does, think about those confusing times in your life, when you seemed overwhelmed by conflicting or growing responsibilities. It's almost as if you were in a whirlpool, all those responsibilities swirling about you, a blur of time and movement. At such moments, time seems to be moving faster, so fast you feel unable to act. In essence, things are out of control.

Kids feel this way quite often. They often move from one whirlpool to another. They have a whirlpool of popularity and social acceptance, another of school work and future planning. They have a whirlpool of growing independence and all the attending conflicts with mom and dad. And they have the whirlpool of their own adolescence, a time some psychologists refer to as "physiological insanity," characterized by rampant hormones and desperate cries for attention.

It's no wonder that sometimes they feel unable to act. Even when they do act, they act impulsively. The child who learns to focus on each of his or her responsibilities, like the good athlete, learns to slow down time. When children slow down time, they react to things less impulsively. And when they react less impulsively, their lives are more balanced and consistent.

Stay Within Yourself

When athletes are cool-headed, they are able to self-regulate their levels of intensity. They know that when they get too excited, they tense up. Their muscles get tight, and they fail to perform smoothly and effortlessly. When athletes try too hard, they overextend themselves. The prospect of having to make the game-winning free throw can cause a basketball player's muscles to tighten up so severely, he or she can barely raise the ball, let alone shoot it smoothly and accurately.

Coaches understand, then, that they must not push their athletes too hard or expect too much of them. "Stay within yourself" is a common catch phrase. "I don't expect miracles from you. Just give me your best effort. That's all I can ask and that's all you can do. If you do that, both of us will be satisfied." Again, it's a matter of expecting the proper effort. "Don't talk to me about winning or losing; just try your hardest. That's all I want."

Just as the good coach asks her athletes for a maximum effort, parents ask their teens to do their best. That's really all we *can* ask. There is nothing better than your best, no matter how consistently you try or how hard you dream. A problem with dreaming is that children often compare themselves to others. They see themselves performing beyond their capabilities and often set unrealistic and unachievable standards. At that point, success is impossible.

"Never try too hard" sounds like the wrong thing to say to a kid. But the child who walks into a final exam knowing that he has to get straight-As on his report card may blow the exam. Pressure and tension speed up time and make us "uptight." Uptight kids limit their successful experiences.

Success for children must always be within their reach. And when effort is its own reward, when doing good and being the best you can be are their primary standards for success, children become winners. They enter each day feeling good about themselves, and they end each day feeling a sense of accomplishment. I never expected a halfback with only moderate speed to be a breakaway runner. Similarly, parents can never expect a simply good student to be class valedictorian. Help them to live within themselves and to be happy with what they find there.

Be Positive!

Good coaches teach their athletes to engage in positive self-talk. In other words, when preparing for an important extra point, I wanted our place kicker to visualize and to *feel* the right way to kick the football. I told him to focus only on proper performance and to *expect* a successful kick. I didn't allow kids to think, "If my plant foot is bad, I'm going to shank this thing" or "I've been pulling my kicks all week. I hope I don't now!"

If the last thing the kicker thinks just before his attempt is a week of pulled kicks, you can bet he'll pull this one. That kind of negative self-talk focuses on failure. No matter what he did all week, I wanted him to *believe* that this kick was going to be perfect. I wanted him to learn from those pulled kicks all week and to make whatever corrections were necessary. But then I wanted him to forget them. I would tell my kids often that "you can't 'shoulda'!" Don't say, "I should have done this" or "I should have done that." Just learn from the experience, then forget it and focus on positive expectations.

Francis Bacon once said, "Praise yourself daringly; something always sticks." Teach children to congratulate themselves when they do something well, to expect only the best from their efforts. Teach them to smile as soon as they get up in the morning. Smile yourself at the advent of a new day. Smiles are contagious. They not only light up our children and others, they brighten us. What a marvelous lesson for young people. The world is a happy place whenever we decide to make it so.

Negativity for children, as with athletes, is failure-oriented. The child who enters a final exam expecting to do poorly may not do as poorly as expected but certainly will not do as well as he might. The child who enters school each day expecting to be the butt of everyone's jokes will certainly find a "Kick Me" sign on his back by the end of the day. What we expect is often what we get. Kids must learn to expect the best from each day.

They're not going to find it every day. Sometimes life can be one curve ball—or oddball—after another. Children are going to do poorly on their exams or be picked on once in a while. The point is, if they *expect* to do poorly or to be picked on, they probably will. Children who expect *good* things from life are more likely to find them. They project a more positive outlook, one that enters exams, as well as school, confidently. A supportive atmosphere at home gives children such confidence. And when things go poorly consistently—and they will sometimes—that same support at home will make negative experiences more tolerable.

This supportive atmosphere is critical. I learned that a local coach, just a few months ago, has a lot to learn in this regard. He told one of his receivers as they were getting on the bus for an away game that he would be taken out of the game if he missed the first pass thrown to him. The youngster became immediately uptight, and he stayed that way all the way to the game. And what happened during the game? Of course, he missed the first pass thrown to him.

It is sometimes terrifying to think about the power we have to create self-fulfilling prophecies. If we tell Tom that he can't go out for the weekend if he blows the next test, we've helped create a self-fulfilling prophecy. By focusing on outcome, we've helped Tom blow the test. A better practice is to tell Tom that he can't go out for the weekend if he fails to put *effort* into preparation for the test, then give him nothing but encouragement when test time rolls around.

Finally, as with athletes, kids also must learn that they "can't shoulda." "I should have done better on that quiz," or "I should have gone out for football this year" are comments that lead nowhere. Rather, children must learn to work harder for the next quiz or to join another activity. Fretting over past failures is self-defeating. Learn from them, then forget them. The most important step in life is the next step. Teach your children to make it a good one and to expect positive things from it.

Let the Win Take Care of Itself

Athletes who perform at their best think positively. They also focus on their performance and let the win take care of itself. Good coaches emphasize to players that all they can control is their own performance.

And they recognize that there is a difference between success and winning. Success is mastering yourself, perfecting your fundamentals, committing to your teammates, and making a maximum effort. Winning may or may not follow. I have discovered that it usually does if kids maximize everything else. But it may not. The kids may walk into the locker room without a victory. But they'll still be successful. Good coaches know this, and they teach it to their athletes.

The Harder I Work, The Luckier I Get

This is the mantra of sports teams all over the country. It is a great piece of advice for all of us. Children can't control how well classmates do on tests or whether or not schools continue to engage in silly practices like grading on the curve. All they can control is their effort before the test and their level of motivation at test time.

Like athletes, adolescents must learn the difference between success and winning. They learn quite early that they don't always get straight-As. Their IQ scores are not always the highest in the class. They don't always qualify for admission to the most prestigious colleges in the country. Only a few athletes ever make All-Conference, fewer All-State, fewer yet receive athletic scholarships.

Not everyone has an IQ of 180 or gets into Harvard. Life would get pretty boring if we all did. But what a wonderfully exciting life it would be if we all cared about each other, celebrated our diversity, rejoiced in our individual uniqueness, and tried our best at whatever was important to us. All children can find satisfaction and success in their efforts if they are blessed with parents and teachers who value and routinely recognize character.

When parents and teachers consistently recognize effort (performance) over winning (outcome), children won't feel the need to do whatever it takes to get an A or to get into the "best" schools. These may be worthwhile goals, but the effort put into realizing them is far more important than the outcome. Consistent effort is the key.

* * * * * * *

"Prompting" enables coaches and parents to emphasize each of the characteristics of peak performance: confidence, focus, reasonable motivation, positive thinking, and process rather than outcome. Keep these five characteristics in mind whenever discussing schoolwork or chores around the house. They don't have to be mentioned in any order. You don't even have to include them all. Use as many as possible, however, to encourage your child's peak performance.

Dialogue - Prompting Technique

Coach:	Well, Phil, do you think we'll get the job done today?
Player:	Boy, I know the team's ready. Look at Jerry. He can't wait to get out there. I just hope I don't let everybody down.
Coach:	What? What are you talking about? You're not going to let everybody down.
Player:	I hope not. This is my first start.
Coach:	That's right, and you're starting because you're the best man for the job. You've got a great arm, and you're one of the best leaders on the team. (Instill confidence in player)
Player:	But all that offense! A lot of it is still new to me.
Coach:	Don't worry about that. The game plan focuses on inside belly and power. Focus on them, and the passing attack will be mostly play-action. You know all that. I made sure of it last week. (Promote a sense of focus for athlete)
Player:	But I sure blew a couple plays in Thursday's scrimmage.
Coach:	That's ancient history. You know what you did wrong, and you learned from it. I watched you do it the right way. You know what you have to do today. Forget about last week. Focus on today! (Promote positive thinking and re-establish focus)
Player:	Yeah, this victory is very important to us. If we lose this one, how do we beat Fairfield?
Coach:	Forget Fairfield, and forget any thoughts about losing—or, for that matter, about winning. You have a job to do, and you're the best guy for that job. Concentrate on

COACHING CHARACTER AT HOME

your performance—*only* on your performance. Give me your best shot, and everything else will take care of itself. Relax,
Phil, handle the game one play at a time,
and you'll be just fine! (Emphasize performance over outcome, push for reasonable levels of motivation, and re-emphasize
positive thinking and focus)

PARENT TO CHILD

Child: Boy, this class is going to be a real kick
           today!
Parent: What class?
Child: This crazy accelerated thing in math you
           signed me up for.
Parent: Wait a minute, hot shot. You said you
           wanted to try that class. You signed up for
           it! What's the problem?
Child: It's full of nerds and whiz kids. They're
           gonna kick my academic butt.
Parent: Impossible. Three teachers and some
           great test scores recommended you for
           the class. Admit it, my friend, you just
           happen to be pretty good in math. You
           may have to work a little harder, but
           you're bound to be one of the best in the
           class. (Reaffirm confidence in child)
Child: But there's gonna be a whole lot more
           homework.
Parent: Probably. But that's no problem for you.
           Just do your math first every night. Get it
           all done and then do the rest. Maybe do
           your math before dinner, then the rest
           afterward. (Promote a sense of focus for
           the child)
Child: Yeah, I guess. . . . But what if I blow it?
           I'm gonna look like a real joker.

Parent:	Tom, if you do everything you're supposed to, there's no way you will blow it. And I don't even want you thinking that way. When you walk into that class tomorrow, tell yourself you're as good as anyone else in that room. You are, you know. Then take it all a day at a time. That's all you can do. (Promote positive thinking and re-establish focus)
Child:	Boy! Are the guys gonna howl when I get a D! There goes Mr. Grade Point Average.
Parent:	Forget the grade and forget the grade point average. That's so far in the future, it doesn't even matter. You concentrate on the class a day at a time and give it your best effort. That's more than enough. Relax, will you? The grade will take care of itself—whatever it is. (Emphasize performance over outcome, push for reasonable levels of motivation, and re-emphasize positive thinking and focus)

Let's Wrap It Up

Obviously, helping kids achieve peak performance depends on a whole lot more than one dialogue. Instilling confidence, focus, and positive thinking in kids involves much more than a short conversation before or after school. Peak performance for kids as for athletes results from supportive relationships and a consistent focus on positive behaviors. Help the kids set reasonable and achievable goals, then promote the consistent behaviors that achieve those goals. "Practice, practice, practice."

This chapter focused on individual effort as a key to success. Character is dependent on it, but true character also results from the willingness and the ability to cooperate. Teamwork is more essential for families than for athletic teams. If the boat sinks for one member of the family, everyone goes under. It's to our mutual advantage, therefore, to keep the family boat afloat, well-tended, and on course. This is the focus of the next chapter.

5

COOPERATION
Recognizing That We're All in This Together

Pernell was a 5'9" block of sculptured granite. His appearance was more like a well-muscled pit bull than a Greek god. His dad contracted heavy equipment for construction companies, and Pernell, only seventeen, was already his right-hand man. He also was our starting fullback, an All-Conference selection as a junior, and one of the leading ground gainers on our team.

He almost didn't come out for football during his junior year. When playing for the sophomore team, his coaches insisted that he play guard. He had always wanted to be a fullback, so he decided against football during his junior and senior years. Fortunately, I ran into him while he and his family were vacationing in northern Wisconsin the summer before his junior year. After swapping a few stories about fishing, his earlier problems with the sophomore team, and the football program in general, I asked him one question.

"Do you like football?" He answered "yes," so I told him to come out for the team. "Will I have to play guard?" he asked. "No, you play what you want," I answered, "but if you're not playing a lot, you may have to rethink your decision. But that will be up to you." So Pernell came out for football and became one of the best fullbacks in our school's history. Determination and simple cooperation from someone he came to respect made the difference.

An accident during the summer before Pernell's senior year, however, almost ended his playing career. He had been working with his dad, and the tractor he had been driving ran out of gas. So he backed up one of the trucks, grabbed a piece of hose, and siphoned some gas from the truck into the tractor. In the process, the hose slipped and Pernell inhaled and ingested several ounces of gasoline. He collapsed almost immediately and would have died were it not for the quick thinking of a few of his coworkers.

He was hustled off to the local emergency room, where he received excellent medical attention and the advice to stay in bed for the next four or five days for some rest and continuing diagnosis. After swarms of football players, coaches, and family crowded in and out of his room, he was released with the prognosis that he probably would never play football again because of the damage to his lungs.

Pernell refused to accept the prognosis. So did his family, coaches, and teammates. They were always at his side, patting him on the back and reminding him that the first day of practice was only two months away. At first, he had problems walking up and down the street in front of his house, but, with time, he was walking, then running around the block. Within weeks, he was running around the track at the school, accompanied every time by four or five of his teammates.

Pernell showed up for the first day of practice, executed his assignments, ran wind sprints, and smiled broadly every time a teammate high-fived him after a good run during scrimmage. He felt so good and performed so well that his coaches and teammates decided to call him Motor Man, offering to "fill him up" before every game so we could ride him into the end zone. He became an All-Conference fullback and received offers to play for a few small colleges, but decided instead to go into his dad's business.

Pernell's doctors were convinced that his excellent physical conditioning at the time of the accident helped save his life. His attending physician added, "Pernell's recovery goes well beyond physical conditioning and medicine. Love is a powerful influence. I'm convinced that the doses he received every day did more for him than anything else." I agreed with him. I learned long ago that the willingness to cooperate is not only an expression of trust and caring, but a statement of belief in others, even of love.

What Is Cooperation?

Cooperation is nothing more than working together with others to realize common goals. Sounds simple enough, but the implications are far-reaching. Consider just three characteristics of groups. One, groups can enjoy positive interactions and relationships, or they can be almost totally antagonistic. Two, their purposes can be either positive and worthwhile or negative and destructive. Finally, they can be efficient and effective or little of each.

Cooperation, therefore, can be either good or bad. Groups are good if they work well together toward something worthwhile, not so good if they don't. Some families, for example, work well together; others constantly bicker and fight. Mutual cooperation characterizes the first family, mutual antagonism the other. Experience has taught me that mutual cooperation creates an energy where 1+1=3 or 4. Conversely, mutual antagonism is more like 1+1=0.

Next, consider cohesion, the act of sticking together, of being closely knit. Coaches and parents want their respective groups to stick together, to care about one another and to work together closely. But a sense of purpose is still more important than even the most cohesive group. I had a football team one year that was very closely knit. The kids liked each other, went to parties together, and associated with each other in school and in the community.

One day during practice, I noticed that the drills were going smoother than usual. The kids were blocking and tackling better than ever, but they weren't making any noise. A football field without the sounds of contact is traffic without horns. It just isn't right.

So I stopped practice and, smiling, informed them, "OK, boys, quit the union and start playing football, or we just might run sprints after practice by the light of the silvery moon!" The union? That's a collective agreement among football players during practice to make it look good but to go easy on each other.

Highly cohesive groups will pull such stunts. Anyone who has raised twins knows their genius for chicanery. Strongly knit groups with weak purposes produce very little. Strongly knit groups with strong purposes work miracles. Look at what

Pernell's family and the football team did for Pernell. Look at what the heroes aboard the flight in Pennsylvania did to thwart the terrorists and what the fire and police departments did in New York. There is perhaps no better evidence of cohesion and a sense of purpose.

Cooperation and commitment—a formula for sure-fire success, as long as commitment comes first. And I've already indicated that the most binding commitments are made by kids who feel responsible for making them.

With our help, kids must select the areas in which they want to make commitments, then make them—without coercion or parental control. This sounds like a big order, but it's easier than you might expect, synthesized in one important piece of advice: To secure your children's cooperation, *control the processes by which they make decisions and don't make all the decisions for them.* Because this advice is so critical, a sample dialogue is provided.

* * * * * * *

Sometimes kids want to do things that come as a complete shock to us. Some coaches and parents are inclined to dismiss such wishes with an "I know better" attitude. Such a response from adults can create resentment in many kids, compromising their commitment and undermining their willingness to cooperate.

Even when we *do* know better, it's sometimes wise to allow kids to make decisions, even bad decisions. Good coaches and parents may not know all the right answers, but they do ask the right questions.

Obviously, if the decision is so bad that it hurts the team, coaches will deny it, but usually with a good explanation. At other times, even if the decision is ill-advised, good coaches will go along with it, recognizing that most kids will never be satisfied until they get a chance to prove themselves. Providing the chance keeps the athlete's motivation high, even if the decision eventually proves to be wrong.

The key for coaches, as for parents, is to permit the decision *but within the framework required by the coach.* Such a framework includes reasonable expectations and good accountability. It also involves a process controlled by the coach, usually a series of questions that result in an understanding of the conditions within which the decision can be made. Notice how the coach does it in the following dialogue.

Dialogue - Shaping

Player: I want to play center because I think I'll play more. I might even make first-team.

Coach: This is news to me, Sally. I thought you liked forward. You're second-team, but you've been playing quite a bit.

Player: I know, but I think I can start at center.

Coach: You've never played with your back to the basket. That's a whole different game, kiddo.

Player: Yeah, I know, but if Rachel and Maureen can do it, I think I can, too.

Coach: Well, maybe we ought to give it a try, but keep in mind that if one of the sophomores plays your forward position well, you might not be able to get it back if center doesn't work out for you. (Start introducing consequences of the athlete's decision)

Player: (Hesitatingly) Oh, yeah. . . . But I really think I can play center.

Coach: Maybe you can; you're a good athlete. So give it a try, but maybe you ought to think about the time factor. How much time will you need to know if this decision was a good one? (Oversee the process by controlling the conditions of the decision)

Player: I should know in a week and a half to two weeks.

Coach: OK, let's call it two weeks. You'll start playing center tonight at practice. Oh, but what if we really need you to play forward in one or more of the next few games? You know, Colleen could get hurt. (Control more of the conditions of the decision)

Player: (A bit more excited) Oh, sure, I'd do that.

Coach:	Good. Sounds like we're all set. Oh, one more point. What will have to happen by the end of the two weeks for both of us to know that you made the right decision? (Control more of the conditions of the decision)
Player:	Well, if I'm not starting or playing more at center, I'll go back to forward.
Coach:	Sounds good, Sally. Go for it.

PARENT TO CHILD

Child:	But I need more money, Dad. I might even want to buy a car.
Parent:	Yeah, yeah, I felt the same way when I was your age. Of course, back then we were still driving a horse and buggy!
Child:	Yeah, I know, and you had to walk fifteen miles through the snow to get to school.
Parent:	No, only ten. But about this job. What are you talking about?
Child:	The Squiggly Wiggly needs a stock boy every day after school and on some weekends. I can make seven bucks an hour.
Parent:	Hmm, every day and on weekends. Pretty big time commitment. Share your thoughts with me about the amount of time it will take. (Control the process by asking the right questions. This is a presupposition statement. It is complimentary to the child in the sense that it presupposes that he has given preliminary thought to the consequences of the decision.)
Child:	No sweat. I'm figuring maybe three hours a day after school. The track team does that much.
Parent:	True enough, but what about weekends?

Child:	It'll probably be either Saturday or Sunday every weekend.
Parent:	OK. Now let's see if I have this right. We don't want *both* days every weekend and *fewer* days during the week because a popular young fella like you needs time to share his charms with friends. Did I get it right? (Use humor to start exploring other alternatives)
Child:	Hey, Dad, that ten miles a day through snow worked for you! What would all the girls do without me?
Parent:	Right, but let's revisit the same amount of time as the track team. How many of your friends on the track team are struggling with trig? How do you plan to handle that? (Another presupposition question but one that provides some parent control)
Child:	I don't know; I'll find time after work.
Parent:	Correct me if I'm wrong, but you have time right now, and you're still struggling. Didn't you promise your mom a couple days ago that trig would improve? How did you plan to do that?
Child:	Tutor, maybe see my teacher once in a while. . . . OK. I see where this is going. Maybe I should try for every other day during the week and cool it on weekends. How does that sound?
Parent:	Hey, guy, it's your grade. How does it sound to *you*? (Keep the ownership with the child but maintain control of the process)
Child:	I can do it.
Parent:	OK. How will we know if you *don't*? (Maintain control of the parameters of the decision)

Child: My grade won't go up. I have a big test in two weeks. I'll know then.

Parent: You're doing well in your other courses, so I'm assuming that a part of your plan is to keep them where they're at. (Control more parameters of the decision)

Child: You got it. I can buy that.

Parent: OK, as I hear it, you will work every other day during the week, your trig grade will improve, and your other grades will stay where they're at. Is that what I heard? (More process control)

Child: Yeah.

Parent: And if the grades slip?

Child: I'll quit the job.

Parent: Go for it, Moneybags.

Four Characteristics of Cooperation

Sports psychologists Albert Carron, M. E. Shaw, and A. Zander identified four characteristics for developing closely knit groups:

- Proximity: A sense of closeness and togetherness.
- Distinctiveness: A sense of uniqueness and belonging.
- Similarity: A shared purpose that transcends differences.
- Group goals and rewards: A willingness to put the success of the group ahead of personal gain.

Good coaches have used them for years to create closely knit teams. Just as parents use dialoguing techniques like Shaping, they can create a closely knit group of the family by accommodating these four characteristics.

HOW COACHES ACHIEVE COOPERATION:

Proximity: Let's Stick Together

Athletes are necessarily in close physical contact most of the time. Although this can cause an occasional problem, such as hassles in the locker room, it almost always promotes bonding. Athletes spend time together in the locker room, the training room, in team meetings, the weight room, on the bus, on the practice field or court. At such times, interaction and a sense of togetherness are unavoidable. So is cooperation. This is especially true when coaches encourage mutual caring and remind them of their common goals.

Distinctiveness: We Really Are Special

To most good coaches, distinctiveness results from two things—hard work and sacrifice. If their athletic experience is really worthwhile, all kids learn to pay the price, to sacrifice something to earn that feeling of being special. Distinctiveness doesn't come easily. Kids have to work for it. That's why many coaches, myself included, praise the kids every year for their willingness to do what most other students are unable or unwilling to do.

I reminded them often that "specialness" had nothing to do with being football heroes. They were special because they had the guts to enter the arena. Any pride they earned related to their ability and the willingness to work hard, to risk pain, to sacrifice for the good of the team, to make maximum efforts, and to deny themselves the pleasures that routinely tempt other kids. Youngsters who cooperate with their teammates and coaches to honor such commitments really are special.

Similarity: We're in It for the Same Things

I created a slogan for a team one year that became a catch phrase during the season. "One family—one destiny." It synthesized everything this particular team represented and what they wanted for the year. I had them identify specific team goals in the beginning of the year. They created goals like "Make a total effort every practice," "Help each other," "Cooperate with the coaches," and "Attend every practice." I wrote the goals on the blackboard as the team agreed on them, then made copies of them for distribution the next day.

I also posted the motto over the locker room door, in the training room, and over the door that exited onto the field. Every time the kids started bickering in practice or slacking off during drills, I reminded them of their goals. Sometimes I even re-explained what "One family—one destiny" meant to all of us: mutual cooperation, shared support, and similarity of purpose.

Most athletic teams consist of a range of personalities, abilities, and ethnic, racial, religious, and economic backgrounds. Good coaches understand that cooperation among them requires a similarity of purpose that transcends color and race and that introduces an element of family that some of them might not find at home. Even if it is evident at home, a sense of family promotes bonds that improve team performance and behavior, both on and off the field or court.

Group Goals and Rewards: Everybody Makes a Contribution!

When coaches want to develop a sense of family and cooperation among teammates, group goals and rewards are considerably more important than individual honors. Standout performers are going to get their share of recognition. Given the broad reach of the media, such recognition is unavoidable, and sometimes it's excessive.

Media mongers aren't interested in the tall, skinny youngster on the fourth team who has more heart than talent. *Good coaches are.* They recognize that blue chippers may be the arms and legs of a team but that the gutsy little kid who accepts daily punishment during practice and never gets in a game is its heart and soul. That's why good coaches recognize effort, not just accomplishment. And that's why we have a special fondness for those little also-rans who exhaust themselves every day for the good of the team. They won't be also-rans for long.

How Parents Achieve Cooperation:

Proximity: Time Together Pays Dividends

Families have more opportunities for close physical contact than most athletic teams. We may spread in several different directions every morning and the kids may be involved in everything from softball to hard rock after school, but we all return to the same home base every night. This re-gathering represents golden moments for smart parents. Such moments are opportunities to dine, talk, and play together, to share special moments in the day, and to help resolve problems.

Togetherness is our top priority. Certainly we also understand that the very after-school activities we seek for our children to promote their growth can become major interferences to the need to pray and play together. I'm the first to defend sports and activities programs after school for kids, but I'm also quick to suggest that, as with everything else in our lives, we have to establish priorities. Experience with my own three daughters has taught me that togetherness at home was my family's number one priority.

There is nothing more important in the lives of children than to share special moments with their parents. Such moments can last a lifetime—as precious memories or as threads in the fabric of what we become as adults. Famed poet William Wordsworth suggested, "The child is father of the man." What we are as children will determine what we become as adults. In essence, beloved, cherished children become beloved, cherished adults. Proximity develops the cooperation that helps create such relationships.

Distinctiveness: Every Child Must Learn to Stand Tall

Every child, in as many ways as possible, must be distinct, consciously different from everyone else on earth. Vinnie Barbarino, that underachieving lover boy on the old sitcom *Welcome Back, Kotter* once advised his fellow under-achievers, "You've got to feel *who you are!*" The audience laughed at Vinnie's hair-tossing strut across the stage as he delivered the line, but it was marvelous advice. Kids spend most of their early lives trying desperately to find out who they are. Sometimes the search lasts into adulthood.

What many of us fail to realize is that the answers are found in our own backyards and are shaped by the cooperative spirit of family members and friends. I don't have to travel abroad to discover that I am a worthwhile person. All I need is someone in my life to help me pay the price, to *earn* the satisfaction of knowing who I am.

Similarity: Let's Join Hearts and Hands

Dinners together, family vacations, photographs of generations of family members displayed prominently in the house, family meetings, shared charitable activities, cooperative chores around the house, reciprocal interest in each other's activities, and professed pride in who we are as a family all highlight similarities and promote cooperation among family members. The key for parents is to balance the distinctiveness as discussed in the previous section with the similarities suggested in this one.

Group Goals and Rewards

"Us" is always better than "me." Such balance is achieved by once again heeding the advice of Kahlil Gibran: "Let there be spaces in our togetherness." In other words, families must be close and maintain a focus on their similarities, but they must also nourish the elements in their personalities that make them unique. Individual accomplishment is important, but, to guarantee cooperation in the family, group goals and rewards are most important.

Don't encourage your kids to compete with each other. Certainly parents want their kids to do marvelous things individually, but most avoid motivating them by pitting them against each other. Someone is going to lose such a competition, and we want each of our kids to win as often as possible. Winning is easier when a child's only competitor is herself. It's a healthy competition that the child is highly motivated to win.

The same is true of family goals and rewards. If the kids help develop the goals and choose the rewards, they'll commit to them. And what kinds of goals should we help them target? The very same ones athletes target for a successful season. They should want to make a total effort every day, help each other, and cooperate with their parents and siblings. Every family can achieve these kinds of goals. Every child can make a valuable contribution.

When you see the kids working toward a goal, recognize them immediately with specific comments: "You did a nice job helping Cindy with her homework last night. Your comments about how to understand and use participial phrases really helped her." Or "Tom, I want you to know how much I appreciated your help with the backyard yesterday. I know that you were done with your chores, and I was running out of gas. You were a lifesaver."

Such comments eventually will eliminate the need for family outings or for trips to Herbie's Pizza Playground as rewards. Specific recognition helps kids understand that the performance of a good deed is, in fact, its own reward. Psychologists call it functional autonomy. You and I will call it *feeling good* because of *doing good*. Once kids reach this point, positive behaviors become habits, and external rewards are no longer necessary.

The Essentials of Cooperation

By nature, kids are not cooperative. Materialism and the self-indulgent myopia of countless numbers of young people promote the me-first mentality that divides us and effectively weakens our resolve as families and communities. Good coaches don't permit this.

"Put on your game face, stand tall, and do your job" are the demands of good coaches. When kids respond accordingly, they win. They win at everything they do—for one simple reason. They have character. They are quality people. They have no time for trash talk; they're too busy doing their jobs.

Here are some essential maxims for teaching cooperation on the playing field and in our homes.

I Am My Brother's Keeper

Cooperation and teamwork are impossible without mutual respect and an unconditional willingness to help each other. As the old saying goes, "There is no 'I' in team." Good coaches understand that the team with mutual respect is a winner. Legendary coach Bobby Bowden, one of the winningest football coaches in NCAA history, emphasizes the concept of mutual respect and teamwork by telling his players to "Hold the Rope!"

He tells them that if we all hold the rope and pull our weight, we're going to win our share of games. When times get tough during difficult games, his players remind each other to "Hold the Rope!" It's a simple term, but it communicates everything each player must do to share the burden of responsibility. It's a phrase that tells the entire team to disregard their individual differences and to focus on common goals. Isn't that a good definition of love? Love isn't just looking at each other. It's two or more people looking in the same direction.

Opinions That Differ From Mine Are Invaluable to Me

Good coaches don't want to be surrounded by yes men. If six coaches agree on every issue involving strategy, five coaches are unnecessary. I always felt that I was closing in on perfection every time I admitted my imperfections, and I have a lot of them. Recognizing them forced me to listen to others, which invariably got me closer to the truth. Whenever I got closer to the truth by listening to the differing opinions of my fellow coaches and players, we won more games. Good coaches understand this and purposely seek out divergent opinions. Sometimes it's the most outlandish idea that eventually wins the contest.

The Person Who Can't Change His Mind Can't Change Anything

Resilience *and* flexibility. Nothing worthwhile was ever achieved without them, and real cooperation depends on them. "If that way doesn't work, find another way!" "If you've been doing it the same way forever, it's time to find a new way." Good coaches understand that the ability to adapt to disruption or changing circumstances eventually brings success. If things aren't going our way, and we fail to adapt, we lose. If we make the necessary adjustments, we improve our chances, especially if we believe in the adjustments. Sometimes just this belief in them brings success.

Always Discipline With Dignity

Never strip young people of their dignity, no matter how angry they make you. Good coaches realize that directing anger at players can have the opposite effect we intend, especially if we destroy their dignity in the process. Dignity is a shield that protects self-esteem. Break it down, and the child's self-confidence suffers; and, when that happens, his or her performance falls apart. That's the last thing good coaches want from their athletes.

More to the point, the angry and demanding coach creates resentment among players. When kids are resentful, they blame the coach's anger rather than their own actions for their poor performance. They start mumbling: "How can anyone play for her; all she does is scream." Or "No wonder I'm missing lay-ups; I can't even think straight with that clown yelling all the time." Peak performance results from an athlete's ability to self-evaluate and to cooperate with coaches and teammates. He won't do either if he's blaming the coach for his poor performance.

Respect Is a Two-Way Street

Every parent wants, even demands respect from his or her children. Kids expect the same thing from their parents.

Respect is communicated not only in what we say but in how we say it. It is a matter of attitude, behavior, and tone of voice. Parents can be pretty direct, even pointed with kids if they smile and speak softly. All of us assume that people who don't yell at us must respect us.

Rapport is important. For that matter, psychologists tell us that we are in rapport—enjoying an agreeable and harmonious relationship—when we speak in the same voice tones and gesture the same way. Rapport is critical in every relationship, especially in the family. What is important for parents to remember is that we may not be in complete agreement about issues with the kids, but we can maintain rapport by being careful about our tone of voice and body language.

Unconditional love is more important. A friend once asked me what it's like having grandkids. I told him that being a grandparent is probably your one best shot at unconditional love. I guess I still agree with the substance of that statement, but I've learned a little more over the years. Now, I'm sure that unconditional love is possible in every relationship, even in one with kids who are in the throes of the physiological insanity of adolescence!

I've learned that unconditional love is demonstrated every time we separate the child from his or her actions. "Sometimes I may really dislike what you do, but I always, always love *you*." We get into trouble in our relationships with kids, even with most adults, when we confuse what they do with who they are. When we keep the two separate, demonstrated respect is much easier.

Love is not a reward. Furthermore, respect is demonstrated consistently when we avoid giving love as a reward. Love is not a bargaining chip or a seal of approval. Good coaches and good parents understand that it's a given, something to be taken for granted in relationships. This is true whether we're on the practice field or in the living room. John Ruskin said it: "When love and skill work together—expect a masterpiece." That's what we want our kids to be—masterpieces. The love part is easy; the skill part is almost as easy.

Welcome Each Child's Uniqueness
Each child's perspective is unique, sometimes so unique we can barely see them on the other side of the generation gap.

But the very differences that seem to separate us not only energize our relationships but give them the depth that makes life more interesting and fulfilling.

Kids are not lowercase versions of their parents. Knowing that, good parents learn to celebrate differences, even to invite them because the very things that seem to separate us often have the greatest power to strengthen the family's adaptability.

Certainly, we influence our children's values. It would be impossible for us not to. But we must be careful to welcome their uniqueness as we welcome strangers to our homes, with respect, curiosity, and a sincere desire to learn more about them. When we respond to our children this way, we avoid many of the conflicts and tensions some parents find in family relationships.

An Obstacle to Some Is a Stepping Stone to Others

Scores of business and educational researchers are exploring the concept of personal and organizational resilience. "What is it," they ask, "that enables some people to snap back from adversity while others stumble?" Good coaches and parents know the answer. Character. That's why it's so important to any sports program or to any family. Teaching kids to listen is one of the best ways to promote cooperation and character.

I was asked by the coach of my former high school one year to accompany him and his team to a mid-season game. I jumped at the chance. After the game, which they won, we returned to the school for a quick post-game meeting. Coach Lenti asked me to say a few words to the team, and I was immediately shocked by their reaction to me.

I walked to the front of the locker room and was quietly amazed that every eye was on me, their faces expressionless but intent. I gave a short speech, thanked them, and leaned against one of the walls until the meeting ended. As the kids filed from the room to take their showers and Coach Lenti approached me, I told him how impressed I was with the behavior of his kids. "Oh, they learn that early on," he said. "The seniors even remind the younger kids to keep quiet when someone is talking to them. Cooperation and consideration make us listeners, and listeners are learners—and learners are winners."

Wow. That about wrapped it up. This particular coach also reminds his kids that listeners learn more and prepare better. He tells them in the beginning of every season that Lady Luck favors people who are prepared. "Luck doesn't go around looking for just any unprepared clown," he reminds them. "So if you want to follow the path of least *persistence*, don't expect luck to work for you. Listen, be ready, and luck will find *you*."

Listening is a good way to express love. Good advice. You listen to your kids, then be sure they listen to you. How well you listen to them is the key. One thing about kids is for sure. They may not do as we say all the time, but they always do as we *do*. So you listen to them, and they'll start listening to you. And when they do, they won't be able to help noticing your unconditional love, the feedback you share with them about their behavior, and the expectations you and the rest of the family have of each other.

Children who understand expectations, learn to control their behavior, and enjoy the confidence that comes from unconditional love are resilient. They learn to cooperate and to adjust to disruption; they communicate; and they become life-long learners. As such, they never experience the shortsightedness that results from a purely permissive environment. Kids who believe that the world owes them a living invariably fall short. They are excellent examples of Coach Lou Holtz's observation, "The person who complains about the way the ball bounces is likely the one who dropped it."

. . . As They Would Do Unto You

We don't want our kids to drop the ball; we also want them to treat us as we treat them. That rule is golden for a variety of reasons. Unfortunately, some parents are surprised when their kids do exactly that! Some kids treat their parents as they are treated. Let's admit it, sometimes we treat our kids with something less than total respect. We don't do it purposely; it's an insidious kind of thing.

Kids sometimes say and do the wrong things because of the developmental tangle of their own adolescence. Well, we adults have our own tangles. Working, raising kids, maintaining a household, caring for our parents, relating to friends, even dealing with the senseless violence and evil that is affecting so much of the world all take a toll on us. Life is increasingly complicated in our world, and sometimes we slip when it comes to relating to our kids the right way.

Kids need a sense of dignity. Fortunately, it is a problem easily solved. Good parents aren't afraid to look in a mirror once in a while to rearrange elements of their lives. Let's admit it; sometimes we get out of line. When we do, a simple apology and a renewed attempt to do the right thing can get family relationships back on track. An apology dignifies the person who receives it. Our children deserve a sense of dignity and the confidence that accompanies it. Confident athletes perform better; so do kids.

Most important, when shared dignity shapes our relationships with our children, we respond to their behavior in the right ways. For example, if external discipline becomes necessary, we deal with it appropriately—when we are at our best, not when uncontrolled anger and frustration provoke unreasonable and potentially destructive responses. Only a controlled and anger-free reaction to a child's misbehavior promotes the cooperation we want from him to alter that behavior.

Don't give them a chance to blame you. Remember what all good coaches have learned. Our periodic ranting and raving influences kids to blame their performance—or lack of it—on *our* behavior, not on theirs! "My dad has me on edge all the time; how can I possibly study?" or "How can I want to study with Mom yelling all the time?" Mom may not even be yelling all the time, but if the child *thinks* she is, it has the same effect. Kids can blow things out of proportion faster than sports reporters can screw up statistics. Don't give them the chance. Keep your cool and they'll keep theirs. Cooperation is the result.

The Importance of *COOP*

Whenever our coaching staff wanted to promote cooperation, we always kept the term *COOP* in mind. COOP served as a constant reminder for us to do what had to be done to maintain a sense of harmony and cooperation within the team. It works for families, too. The term reminded us to promote and recognize Collective identity, Open communication, Outstanding performance, and Positive expectations.

Collective Identity Emphasizes Togetherness

A collective identity is essential if family members are to cooperate with each other. Bill Cosby once told his misbehaving son that, if he didn't square himself away, his mother would "take him out." He then said, "We can make another one that looks just like you." Isn't that what families are, groups of people who look alike, think alike, and usually behave alike? This collective identity, while at times a source of trouble, is the family's greatest strength. If emphasized positively, it binds everyone to a sense of common purpose.

And, just as athletes must subordinate their need for individual recognition to team goals, everyone in the family must forego the expectation of recognition or reward. The parent who teaches children to do the right thing without expectation of recognition teaches a valuable lesson.

The outside world often forces us to think in terms of "my needs," "my school," "my car," and "my future." The inside world, especially the world of the good family, helps us think in terms of "our family," "our help," "our goals," and "our love." Thinking in terms of "we" instead of "me" opens us up and lets others in.

As parents, we drop our egos and become more open, less guarded, and less fearful. Unconditional love and trust open us up and promote a bold acceptance of the unpredictability of life and give us confidence that the collective and cooperative identity of the family will help resolve whatever problems come our way. Our children learn to approach life the same way, and they experience the contentment that accompanies a caring and open acceptance of what life has to offer. Cooperation at such times is unavoidable.

Open Communication Keeps the Channels Flowing

Communication must be ongoing, free-flowing, open, and honest. Common purposes are unachievable if family members fail to understand that communication is a two-way street. We not only speak; we listen. Parents must model good listening by being alert for not only *what* the child says but *why*.

A child may say to a parent, "You're glued to that television every Saturday." Instead of saying, "Yeah, great games on today," the parent might respond, "What are you saying, Tom? Maybe we don't do enough together." Such an exploration of the *why* behind the child's comment could help deepen family communication, resolve an immediate problem, and avoid future misunderstandings. The key for parents is to listen to the *what*, *how*, and *why* of a child's communication.

Just as important, parents should recognize that sometimes we communicate *too much*. Some of us tend to over-moralize when correcting misbehavior. A preachy, quasi-nagging lecture pushes many kids beyond discomfort into sullen anger. They become resentful because they interpret the approach as a threat to their self-esteem. This is not to say that we must never share the reasons for our concern, but "beating the issue to death" is almost always counterproductive.

Outstanding Performance: No One Has the Starring Role!

Athletes have important roles to perform to assure the success of the team. So do family members. They have roles to perform to promote healthy and happy relationships and to assure the viability of the family. Like athletes, family members must understand their roles, accept them, and perform them correctly. The understanding, acceptance, and performance of roles is essential if the family is to be successful. But this brings up an interesting question: What is a successful family?

The answer to this question may not come immediately to you. As such, it should be obvious that our society has taken little time to answer it. Many people, then, tend to behave within the dictionary definition of a family: a group of people related by blood or marriage. Such a definition is incomplete and provides no indication of roles to perform or standards to measure success.

So this suggests yet another question, one that you may find equally perplexing: Exactly what are the roles we perform as family members? Fortunately, the roles of Mom and Dad are still relatively clear. They may vary somewhat based on the composition of the family, but parents are still expected to provide the physical, social, and emotional means that assure the family's growth and survival. Even this general definition of parental roles is filled with nuances of meaning, but it remains a good starting point.

How, then, do we begin to define the role of son or daughter? Think about it, until families define such roles for themselves, children will never understand, accept, and perform the roles successfully. And the failure to do so will continue to damage families and, by extension, social relationships. Obviously, aspects of such roles are influenced by family circumstances. The death or absence of a parent, for example, thrusts additional responsibilities on one or more children in the family.

Children within different families may be expected, therefore, to perform a variety of different roles. But the basic role of each child in the family is still to develop positively, to become responsible, caring, and supportive, in essence to learn and mature into the roles their parents and other responsible citizens of our country now perform. This means that I, as a parent, must be careful to perform my role well—because my kids are watching! How eagerly I accept my role and how well I perform it will influence how well my children will perform theirs.

Like the good coach, parents must look beyond this occasional frustration and anger to make sure their children understand their roles, accept them, and perform them well. It is a never-ending job. Each stage of growth negotiated by children brings its own special set of new challenges. As a youngster moves from childhood in elementary school to full-blown pubescence in high school, he or she needs the same behavioral refinement. That's where good coaches and parents come in.

As expressed in the introduction of this book, that's the time to "coach 'em." We must teach them the roles they are expected to perform and have the patience and wherewithal to get them to understand, accept, and perform these roles, even as the function of individual roles may change as the child matures. Fortunately, we all can do this. All it takes is time and love. Notice the strategies in the dialoguing technique: Role Clarifying. It follows the next subsection.

Positive Expectations: Focus on the Good Stuff

"Catch 'em being good" has been emphasized recurrently in this book. Good coaches don't try to appear smarter by catching and correcting all the mistakes their kids make. They recognize positive performance first.

Expect success. Kids who expect success think positively and believe in themselves. One of my favorite stories illustrates this. Midway through the season, I was heading out to practice for our regular Wednesday scrimmage, when my starting halfback sidled up next to me and said very matter-of-factly, "No one's going to tackle me today." Surprised, I said, "*No* one?" "That's right," he said. "It's just not gonna to happen." Then, he smiled and jogged ahead of me to join his teammates. I couldn't help but smile. That was just one of the reasons why I loved that kid.

The first time he carried the ball in the scrimmage, he picked up some pretty good yardage but was dragged down from behind by a linebacker. He slapped the linebacker on the back, told him, "Nice tackle," and then headed back to the huddle. Passing me, he said, again very matter-of-factly, "Don't worry; it won't happen again." Well, obviously, it did happen again, in fact quite often. I had almost forgotten his prediction when, some twenty minutes later, he broke through the line for about sixty yards and a touchdown. Jogging back to the huddle, he tossed me the ball, and said, "Told you."

A head game? Maybe, but what's wrong with that? Here was a young man who believed in himself, who was convinced that he could do what he set out to do. And he knew that I believed in him too. What's more, he wasn't bothered by occasional failure. For a full twenty minutes of our scrimmage, he *was* tackled, whenever he ran the ball. But he got off the ground each time with a persistent and positive belief in himself, and his persistence paid off. It always does.

Kids must learn to *expect* success, and parents must help them. This is not to suggest that all they require is the willingness to toss their hats into the arena and success is assured. We all know that life has a way of stomping all over our hats. What it does suggest is that the kids themselves should jump into the arena and learn the value of hard work and commitment. And when they do, they and everyone around them should expect success.

* * * * * * *

Athletes must understand their roles as members of a team, and adolescents must understand their roles as members of a family. Such roles must be explained to them, sometimes repeatedly. Without such explanations, kids lack direction and, invariably, fail to perform within their parents' expectations. Such failure is often the fault of the parent who mistakenly assumes that the child knows what is expected. Role clarifying is an ongoing process in families, just as it is on athletic teams:

Dialogue - Role Clarifying

COACH TO PLAYER

Player:	This doesn't even *feel* like basketball.
Coach:	Why? What's the problem, Don?
Player:	I'd like to touch the ball once in a while.
Coach:	Yeah, I know what you mean, but we've got scorers and ball handlers. We need defenders, and you're the best we've got.
Player:	Thanks, Coach, but I can score, too, you know.
Coach:	You're right, and you'll still do your share, but Phil and Pat can fill it up, can't they?
Player:	Yeah, I can't deny that.
Coach:	Look at it this way. Every time you shut down the other team's high scorer, it's like you're scoring points for us.
Player:	Yeah, I guess. I have to admit that I do like defense.
Coach:	Well then, let's keep focusing on it. Your primary job is going to be to guard their best scorer, unless he's the center, and then we'll have you drop back on him to pressure him from the outside. But at such times, we'll also have you guard their second best scorer. In other words, you're going to be our defensive specialist. How does that sound? Make sense? (Be sure the player understands his role)
Player:	Yeah. You know what? I like the challenge.
Coach:	Then I assume that you like the idea? (Be sure the player accepts his role)
Player:	Yes.
Coach:	OK, we'll check it out this week. You're going to guard Milligan. Let's see how close you get to shutting him down. (Help motivate the player's performance)

PARENT TO CHILD

Child:	Come on, Mom, this is the first time Jessica's parents have asked me over for dinner. I'm only a step or two away from becoming one of the family.
Parent:	Hold on, lover boy, you're a junior in high school. You can't even handle this family, and, believe me, we want you more than they do.
Child:	Of course you do, but you have to admit—I'm easy to love.
Parent:	Well, maybe every other day, and, fortunately for you, today's one of the days.
Child:	Come on, let it be tomorrow.
Parent:	Nope, your grandparents are coming today, and they're staying for dinner tonight. They're expecting to see you and, frankly, your Dad and I expect you to be here. (Use expecting technique; being available to grandparents is a non-negotiable)
Child:	OK, then you tell me what to do about Jessica.
Parent:	You'll figure something out. That's one of the advantages of being so charming. (Use returning technique; keep the ball in his court)
Child:	But Nana would understand. She'd let me go.
Parent:	Sure she would. That's Nana's job—letting you do anything you want. She's good at it. But your job is to love her, too. That's what families do. (Be sure the child understands his role)
Child:	Nana knows I love her.
Parent:	She sure does—because you prove it every once in a while. Aren't you lucky? Here's another chance.

Child: OK, OK, I guess Jessica's loss is Nana's— and Pop Pop's—gain.

Parent: You got it. Sounds to me like you're going to be Mr. Perfect Grandson tonight. (Be sure the child accepts his role)

Child: Of course, perfection isn't much of a stretch for me.

Parent: Oh wow, we must be in for quite a display tonight. (Help motivate the child's performance)

Let's Wrap It Up

Rebellion is one of childhood's most important developmental stages. It's a characteristic not only of toddlers but of teens as well. All kids have to go through it. Otherwise, they get tangled in mom's apron strings and parrot her opinions without developing any of their own. Kids can't learn about themselves by simply shutting up. An early coach of mine, tongue wedged firmly in cheek, advised me before practice one day, "Mike, find out what you don't do well—then don't do it." "Yeah, yeah," I said, trying desperately to be equally flippant, but the older I got, the more sense his comment made.

We all need opportunities to discover what we do well and what we don't do well. We can't do that without making mistakes. Yes, we might dupe ourselves into a sense of domestic tranquility if kids made their mistakes in complete silence. But adolescents who don't make mistakes don't learn, and kids who don't learn don't become independent and make commitments. Without commitment, cooperation is impossible.

That's why commitment was examined before cooperation in this book. Kids must believe firmly in something before they can be expected to cooperate. We want kids who think. Cooperation must not be confused with blind obedience. As desirable as it may sound at certain times, blind obedience doesn't build character. Look at it this way. There are two kinds of kids who never develop any character: the child who never obeys—and the child who never does anything else.

Give me the child with a little fire in her eyes who insists on discovering the things "she doesn't do well." I can be sure that, with a little help—maybe a lot—she's moving in the right direction. She is thinking and, because of it, will learn commitment, cooperation, and, in the process, develop a conscience—the subject of the next chapter.

6

CONSCIENCE
Doing the Right Thing

After practice one day, I was passing by the locker room when I heard, "Knock it off!" Then I heard several muffled voices but couldn't make out what they were saying. Again, I heard, "Knock it off! We don't do that stuff around here." More than a little curious, I walked into the locker room and asked, "OK, what's going on?" Andy, the team captain, one of the best quarterbacks I'd ever coached, was standing in the middle of the room. He turned to me and said, "Don't worry, Coach, everything's under control." I said, "It doesn't sound like it." He responded, "Everything's fine. Don't worry; we'll hold it down."

I trusted Andy, so I told everybody to get dressed. I then left the room and headed for my office, still wondering what it was that "we don't do around here." A couple weeks after the season ended, one of the kids Andy was yelling at that day told me what had happened. Five or six of the kids were putting ten dollars apiece into a pool. They had decided that the player who knocked the upcoming opponent's star running back out of the game would get all the money.

Andy had overheard them and quickly put an end to their plans. He taught them a lesson which, apparently, up until then they hadn't learned from our program. Respecting your opponent is more important than beating him. Andy knew that self-respect is impossible without respect for others. Fortunately, he was in the locker room that day to help teach that lesson. He had been one of the first that year to accept the idea that winning and losing are not the only outcomes of a contest. A third alternative—win/win—is perhaps the most desirable outcome because it elevates every competitor in the game.

Andy also taught his teammates a valuable lesson about conscience. Conscience doesn't permit the kind of silliness that tries to knock opponents out of the game. Andy taught them that conscience isn't an after-the-fact kind of thing. We don't have to do wrong to have our consciences kick in. In fact, they are most helpful when they kick in *before* we do wrong, when they *prevent* us from doing something we know is out of line.

The consciences of young people require training. Like their bodies, their consciences must be conditioned by repetition and drill, shaped by the vigilance of a respected someone who genuinely cares about them.

Who better than a loving parent or a trusted coach? Well, maybe there are others, too. The Andys of this world have a larger impact on their peers than they—and we—sometimes realize. We need their help.

What Is Conscience?

The American Heritage dictionary defines conscience as "the awareness of a moral or ethical aspect to one's conduct." It's a definition that suggests a massive undertaking! Teaching morals and ethics to a group of self-involved, hormonally-driven kids who already have diminished opinions of their parents is at the very least a challenge. The challenge becomes even more formidable when we try to get them to *do* what is morally or ethically right. Awareness is one thing; behavior is another.

Getting kids to do what is morally or ethically right is especially difficult when their egos get in the way. The ego, according to most psychologists, is often the servant of our self-indulgence. It makes us feel *entitled*, deserving of the inalienable right to pursue happiness, no matter how illusory, in all its forms. It focuses on our needs and tells us how or when something can be done, but it never tells us if that something is right or wrong, good or bad. That task falls to you and me.

If we handle the task well, our child begins to hear a little voice that sounds an awful lot like us. Fortunately, at least according to cartoonists, we escape detection because the child's conscience looks like an angel sitting on his shoulder. Life still places the occasional demon on the other shoulder, whispering—in the literal sense—sweet nothings in his ear. But, with luck and a lot of work on our part, the angel's voice is more convincing. If really convincing, the child will not only *hear* the right thing to do, but *do* it.

In essence, the child must *know* the right thing to do; and, two, he must feel *compelled* to do it. Good coaches and parents understand, then, that conscience has an emotional as well as an intellectual side. This means that, when he doesn't do the right thing, he feels guilty, out of character, as if his behavior runs contrary to everything he stands for. Such guilt isn't developmentally destructive, just personally disappointing, bothersome. A well-developed conscience, then, is a moral and ethical thermostat that turns up the heat when we get out of line.

Good coaches and parents also understand that if we push kids too hard, the thermostat will force too much heat, creating a morally-driven child who finds guilt around every corner. Such a conscience creates emotional cripples, who are almost as characterless as their unrestrained counterparts.

Our job, then, involves yet another fine line. We want to push kids hard enough to hear and respond to that voice of their conscience, but not so hard that the voice becomes tyrannical in its demands.

A Few Factors
That Influence Conscience

Certainly, conscience has always been important to us, but recent events at home and across the world have challenged the very core of our beliefs about human behavior. As a result, people everywhere are taking a good, hard look at conscience and kids. But are their concerns legitimate? After all, cheating, drinking, talking back, and a range of antisocial behaviors have characterized adolescence since Cain blindsided Abel. So what's the big deal? God knows, there's enough violence in history books and the Bible. Why is today's brand so shocking?

In my mind, it's shocking because kids are killing kids. It's shocking because terrorists have plumbed new depths of evil. What in our society has caused our children to respond so violently to situations that—at another time or in another place—might have provoked only tears or a poke in the nose?

Maybe we can find causes in the widespread rebellion in the '60s and '70s against many of our traditional values. Cries of "If it feels good, do it" that found expression in increasing divorce rates and decreasing sexual restraint are echoed today in the behaviors of movie stars, politicians, and sports superstars. Prominent "role muddles" are teaching our children every day that it's good to be bad. Being bad is a sure-fire way to be noticed.

Or we might consider an unparalleled economic prosperity that permits all of us to satisfy our wants with little regard to our needs, or to the needs of others, here or overseas. Self-indulgence is replacing self-sacrifice; personal freedom is becoming more important than social responsibility. Too many of us are poster boys for a me-first mentality that has established "win at all costs" as the ultimate value. Some of us seek victory at all costs in athletics, schoolwork, and business. Tragically, others of us find it in the sacrifice of innocent people, many of whom are children.

Another cause of significant changes in our behavior is the impact of technology. In many ways, it has created distances between us that many of us seem unable to bridge. It has depersonalized our lives. It seems that our ability to create technology has outdistanced our ability to adjust to it.

The challenge facing coaches and parents, then, is to help our kids overcome these influences and to develop an intellectual and emotional commitment to their own sense of what is right. We won't do it with a permissiveness that accepts good and bad behavior in equal measure, that abandons standards of morality. To good coaches and parents, acceptable moral behavior has few gray areas. That's why we encourage our children not only to actively desire what is good but just as actively to reject what is bad. To develop conscience in our children, we must touch their hearts as well as their minds.

The Recipe for a Good Conscience

Like everything else, conscience is created in an environment. Good coaches understand, for example, that talking about performance doesn't necessarily improve an athlete's execution. They realize that they have to demonstrate and, if possible, model desired performance. Then, they have to get their athletes involved. A good athletic program provides an environment that promotes practice, repetition, observation, evaluation, and improvement.

In addition, consider the athlete's *desire* to perform well. Developing a conscience involves tapping into that desire. As a coach, I knew that my job was not to provide motivation but to cultivate it. Most of the actual motivation I was involved in took place during practice or at other times when I worked hard to meet the needs of my kids. As indicated repeatedly in this book, kids are already motivated—maybe not the same way we are, or even in the same direction—but they have needs that they want to satisfy. Our job is to provide the environment that helps satisfy those needs—and that aligns them with *our* needs and expectations.

Good coaches understand that it is an environment that does much more than inspire players. It engages them. Likewise youngsters can't reflect a commitment to moral behavior by simply *saying* they do. Nor can we as coaches and parents simply *tell* them to listen to their consciences. Our words will be hollow if we have not already shown them how to live. Experience has taught each of us that, contrary to the popular parental ultimatum, kids are going to do as we *do*, not as we *say*. As parents, it's obvious that kids don't listen to us all the time but that they *never fail* to imitate us.

As such, good coaches and parents understand that they, too, must *do* much more than they say. How kids develop a conscience and eventually understand and practice the virtues of self-restraint depend on the willingness of good people to reflect these same virtues in their own behavior and to expect such behavior from their kids. At such times, the focus is off the kids and on *us*, where it belongs. Our kids will never improve unless they have models other than themselves to imitate.

Even more important to remember is this: Only children who are loved know how to love. Kids with poorly developed self-concepts have poorly developed consciences. Only those who feel good about themselves develop the empathy to be morally and ethically sensitive to others. I learned a long time ago to use the word love to define my relationship with my athletes. And I learned to love them without condition or qualification. They got out of line once in a while, but they always knew that I loved them.

The result was stunning. My kids, seeing themselves through the eyes of someone who believed so strongly in them, came to believe more strongly in themselves. Their strong self-concepts resulted in improved self-control and less ego involvement in everything they did. It is these qualities of self-discipline and humility that characterize self-confident people.

HOW COACHES CAN DEVELOP CONSCIENCE:
Taking Another Look at Family

Unconditional love is widespread in sports families. That coaches develop a special fondness for star players is not surprising. What may be surprising is that good coaches love average players even more. Gifted athletes are just doing what comes naturally. Average kids are sacrificing more, working harder, striving harder to overcome limitations, and receiving a lot less recognition from fans and the media. So it doesn't involve a leap of faith to accept the fact that coaches unconditionally love every kid on the team.

Kids with big talent give teams the skills they need to win. Kids with big hearts give teams the character they need to win. The combination is unbeatable. But if I had to choose which of the two I'd rather work with for an entire career, give me kids with big hearts. Talent makes life occasionally sensational. Heart makes it consistently inspirational. I'll take inspirational every time.

Love Is the Greatest Power on Heaven and Earth

What better way to develop positive self-knowledge than to see ourselves as reflected in the eyes of someone who loves us unconditionally? Marriage taught me this lesson. I grew up on the streets of South Chicago, fatherless, usually motherless, marginally civilized, and completely self-focused. The animal within me, a stray dog to local police and teachers, became a center ring performer for high school coaches.

Like thousands, maybe millions of athletes out there, sports defined me. Mike the football player walked confidently through life; the rest of me stumbled almost daily under the weight of a lousy self-concept. Then I met Pat, soon to become my wife. Her unconditional love gave me the strength and courage to find the better me and to become the person she knew I could be.

The Right Choice Is Usually the Toughest Choice

Once children know that they are loved unconditionally, they develop the personality strength to become self-critical. At that point, a consistent conscience is only a few short steps away. Self-criticism requires a knowledge of standards, a willingness to abide by them, and the courage to stick with them in the face of temptation. Training rules are, perhaps, the most visible example of such standards.

We give them two pieces of advice when we first introduce the training rules early in the year. One, temptation can overwhelm reason if we don't have the courage and strength of character to realize that the right decision in life is usually the toughest one. "If it's really a hard one, guys, it's probably the right one!" The youngster who is willing to make the tough choice is a kid with character and a conscience.

Two, all of us have the complete power to choose a course of action, but we don't usually have the power to choose the consequences. That's almost always out of our hands. "So violate the training rules if you must; just be ready to accept the consequences." Coaches like to maintain control, but they know that game situations are in the hands of the players. It's the kids on the field who make the decisions, so coaches make sure that they understand the consequences of bad decisions.

Don't Take Yourself So Seriously

Ego is a hot air balloon. Over-inflated, you fly high, usually just before you fall. The higher you go, the farther you fall. Ego is a sure sign of the need for more emotional and intellectual growth. Humility is easier for us to learn when we know that we are loved unconditionally and have developed the self-knowledge and self-control to beat down our egos. Athletes are no different. A friend of mine, a basketball coach in Chicago, requires his players to do nothing that distinguishes them from everyone else on the team. No names on the jerseys, no facial hair, no unusual shoes, no peculiar hair cuts, nothing that makes them stand out from everyone else. Each player knows his job and how it fits into the team's goals for the season. His responsibility is to perform that job with no special fanfare, recognizing all the while that he is special to his coach. Watching this coach's team is a pleasure. His kids rarely trip over their egos.

HOW PARENTS CAN DEVELOP CONSCIENCE:

Use the Power of the Family

Educational researchers have proven consistently that the quality of parenting is the single best predictor of whether or not a child will get in trouble with the law. They are also confident that the extent of a child's involvement in volunteer activities and the school's extracurricular program are predictors of future success in life. Family, therefore, whether at home or in athletics, is the single most profound influence on children. When that influence is compromised, for whatever reason, outside influences like the peer group and the media fill the void.

Love your kids but expect their obedience. And what is it about the family that makes it such a dominant influence? Well, we know that unconditional love is at the top of the list. Right up there with it? Authority. Parents who establish and explain clear expectations of behavior and expect obedience provide the foundation for their children's future moral and ethical growth. Unconditional love and authority are not mutually exclusive. In fact, they complement each other. Love binds us together, and clear expectations give us direction.

The good news is, love and authority are possible in every family, no matter what its composition and economic circumstances. Unconditional love and expectations of good behavior and obedience flow just as magically from one parent as from two. One parent certainly has a bigger and tougher job, but single parents all over the country are proving that it can be done.

Expect obedience, don't demand it. Good coaches and parents also understand the difference between "authoritative" and "authoritarian." Football great Vince Lombardi, the exemplar of discipline in the sports world, knew the difference. "When those tough sportswriters asked me what made the Packers click, I said 'Love.' It was the kind that means loyalty, teamwork, respecting the dignity of another—heart power, not hate power." *Authoritarian* parents and coaches push children because they need control. "Pushing" makes them feel good. *Authoritative* parents and coaches push, pull, and accompany in equal measure because they love children and want what's best for them.

I have always liked this thought from Albert Camus:

> *Don't walk in front of me;*
> *I may not follow.*
> *Don't walk behind me;*
> *I may not lead.*
> *Just walk beside me*
> *And be my friend.*

It helped guide my behavior as a coach and a parent. I learned quickly that walking beside my players and children resulted in a purposeful loss of control, but that was OK. We were moving in the same direction.

Parents and coaches can be friends without losing their authoritative relationship with their kids. An authoritative relationship involves expectations of behavior and obedience. If such expectations are fair and clearly understood, they are the glue that holds the relationship together. A relationship without expectations is a finely-wrought teacup, pleasing to look at but easily broken and, once broken, very difficult to repair. Relationships built on love and expectations are solid, predictable, not easily broken.

Marvel at the Power of Love

Of the several adventures that characterize childhood, none has more twists and turns or potential pitfalls than the search for an identity. Movies, television, music, magazines, and peer influences flood kids daily with competing identities. The search can be so difficult and the choices so extensive that millions of adults still struggle with the question "Who am I?" One thing is for sure.

As a coach, I saw much the same thing with most of my athletes. Few of the kids who put the pads on for the first time had a sense of their football identities. Who they were as football players was yet to be determined. This identity was revealed to them gradually but consistently during practice or games but never more powerfully than when I or someone else—another coach or player they respected—specifically recognized their improvement or accomplishment. Such accomplishment didn't involve scoring the winning touchdown. More often than not, it involved a maximum effort or the mastery of another skill.

Even when the athlete didn't improve or accomplish something, he knew that I believed he would—sooner or later. Invariably he did. And just think, even more remarkable than the relationships I experienced as a coach are the relationships parents share with their children. Parents exercise an almost magical influence over their children, something far more powerful than even they imagine. *No formative influence in the life of a child is more profound than when the child sees himself reflected in the eyes of a parent who loves him unconditionally.*

Building a Bigger and Better Me

Being loved just as I am—no strings attached, no qualifications—is a rare and treasured experience. It is at the foundation of nearly every religious belief and is central within the thinking of most psychologists. It isn't too surprising, then, the number of coaches who recognize the power of love and are unafraid to express it openly and freely. If tough, demanding coaches are unafraid to hug kids and tell them they love them, why is unqualified love so rare in other areas of our society, even in some of our best homes?

Let's admit it, many of us are afraid. The open expression and demonstration of love leaves us vulnerable. It lets our guard down and permits others to find our soft spots. To some of us, the open expression of love is also a sign of weakness. It makes us look like namby-pamby wimps playing huggy bear with our family and friends. Well, if that's your belief, don't say that to Vince Lombardi or, worse yet, to a New York City fireman. They'll introduce you to new dimensions of huggy bear. The open demonstration of unqualified love cannot be a bad thing. So another question deserves attention. When it comes to the expression or demonstration of unqualified love, what would you do if you weren't afraid? What would you do if these misguided protocols didn't get in your way? The answer is evident: "I'd love more openly." OK, do it! Do what you would do if you weren't afraid, especially in light of the fact that the expression of your unqualified love will make your children unafraid.

The strength they find in your unqualified love will encourage them to take risks, to develop the courage and the self-control to stand up to their peer groups and say no, and to experience the self-love that radiates throughout all their relationships. Children who love themselves are able to love others. What this means is that they develop empathy for the feelings of others and recognize the hurtful and destructive aspects of bullying and belittling. They develop a conscience.

The Incredibly Shrinking Ego

Big egos and too much pride create kids with ravenous appetites for recognition and status. We're well-advised to take a page from my friend's book and be very wary of the externals that feed our children's egos. Kids do themselves a disservice when they define themselves by what they wear or own. Such a superficial preoccupation with "things" retards their personality growth and character development. And when character suffers, so do conscience and humility.

Humility is the one thing in our lives that enables us to overcome pride and develop a conscience. Let me share another story. One year, I had a halfback—let's call him Vic—with eyes in the back of his head. He made cuts in the open field that most kids just dream of. It was a gift, obviously an uncoachable talent, so I couldn't take any credit for it, just stand on the sidelines and smile at the scoreboard every time he scored a touchdown. His talent was so pronounced and he became so dependent on it that he rarely questioned his performance.

As a result, he hit a "performance plateau," a level of execution that certainly was good enough but that didn't even begin to tap all his potential. But as Vic's performance leveled off, his ego continued to grow—bigger and bigger and bigger. I talked to him several times but to no avail. Finally, one day at practice, the guys who were doing all the blocking for him got fed up.

His linemen stopped blocking for him. They gave the appearance of blocking, but they opened wide the door to tacklers. Every time Vic got the ball, he was hit by no fewer than three or four tacklers. It didn't take me long to realize what was happening, so I took him out of the scrimmage and put in another running back. Vic's backup picked up fifteen yards the first time he carried the ball. In fact, every time he ran the ball, he picked up no fewer than five yards.

Finally, I sidled over to Vic and asked softly, "Did you get some kind of a message here?" Obviously angry, he nodded his head. So I said, "Let's talk after practice." Vic and I had several conversations after that practice. He didn't change overnight, but he did change. To his credit, he finally realized that his running ability was useless without blocking. This realization punched some much-needed holes in his ego. As his ego deflated, so did his pride. And as humility replaced pride, he expressed more gratitude to his linemen, reached out more to his teammates, became more self-critical, and became one of the best running backs I ever coached.

A Few Strategies for Developing a Conscience in Kids

That was a tough lesson for Vic. Heaven knows, it was important, but I felt sorry for him that day at practice when his teammates decided to teach it to him. As much as we sometimes want our kids to come down off their high horses, it hurts us almost as much as them when they hit the ground.

Good coaches know that kids who take themselves too seriously tend to emphasize winning over effort and to do most anything that pumps more air into their already over-inflated egos. Ego and the kind of pride that leads to arrogance are insidious viruses that infect teams, sap them of their vitality, and destroy them from within. .

Good parents understand that families are no different. Unfortunately, some parents out there don't make this connection. Some of them are as guilty as their children when it comes to pumping up their egos. How many adults in our society are very bright, very aggressive shadows, insubstantial status-seekers who can't commit to marriage, to the emotional growth of their children, or to a consistent moral or ethical code of behavior? Their lives are consumed in a continuing search for self-gratification. If parents define themselves in this way, so will their kids.

Shared Reflection

Good coaches and parents *demand* moral and ethical behavior. They understand that if they don't stand for something, they'll fall for anything. When kids seem confused about appropriate behavior, therefore, parents must help them reflect on the different behaviors available to them. Such help is critical if children are to move comfortably from one developmental stage to another. The peer group influence of the thirteen-year-old gives way to the strong personal identity of the seventeen-year-old only with parental guidance. It doesn't happen automatically.

The primary strategy to promote growth toward reflection is nothing other than talking to kids. Simple enough. Keep the lines of communication as open as possible. That means frequent dialogues and conscious attempts to draw out the child's real-life problems and to talk about them. It also means sharing stories and experiences at opportune times to get kids thinking. Creative parents do a whole lot of very subtle teaching by sharing off-the-cuff stories at just the right time, usually when kids are struggling with issues they may be reluctant to discuss.

Shared Judgments

Sound judgment depends on the ability to consider different ways to respond to a situation. Again using training rules as an example, I would ask the kids to consider different situations. You're at a weekend party, and one of your teammates asks if you want some pot. How will you respond? What are your alternatives? I would then probe their different answers, pushing them to identify as many alternatives as possible. This would simply be the brainstorming part of the meeting, no one alternative being any better than the others.

The point of this part of the discussion was to have the kids recognize the many different ways to respond to this kind of a situation and to think through each alternative. Learning the art of moral reflection involves, first, recognizing that there are several different ways of behaving in each situation rather than just one. When young people have the opportunity to reflect on certain behaviors *before* they actually encounter them, they are more likely to respond the right way when the real world requires a decision.

During moments of shared reflection, when considering the alternatives available to kids, parents must depend on standards of behavior that have previously been accepted by kids. They must share these values with their children at every opportunity so that they become standards for considering alternatives and making eventual decisions. Without the ability and the opportunity to reflect, kids make poor judgments and, more often, horrendous decisions. Kids have to think about the implications and consequences of alternative ways of behaving, and, when they do, they require a base line of values to guide their thinking.

Opportunities for moral reflection are everywhere. So take time to discuss the evening news with the kids. Ask leading and provocative questions about it: "What do you suppose motivates people to . . . ?" And probe the news by asking hypothetical questions: "I wonder what the heck would happen if . . . ?" Such questions are bait for trolling around the living room. All it takes is one nibble to get everyone hooked on a good discussion.

Shared Decisions
After considering the merits of all the alternatives, I always asked the group to identify the best one. Sometimes there was more than one "best" one, but we always considered why this one or that one was the "best" one. We looked at what values or moral principles helped us decide that it was the best decision. I would then ask the kids to think about what they would *do* specifically after they decided on a "best" course of action. In other words, how will you actually behave? What specifically might you say to your teammate? Knowing the right thing to do and actually doing it often involves knowing a comfortable and effective way to respond.

The situation regarding training rules also involved another important question: What do you plan to do about the fact that it was one of your *teammates* who invited you to use pot? This discussion always took more time. It involved a tougher decision, so often I would ask the kids and their parents to discuss it at home and to share some of their reactions in a future meeting.

When considering alternatives, therefore, parents are advised to help kids consider the consequences of specific alternatives. If I choose this alternative, what are the consequences? How do the consequences of alternative A compare to the consequences of alternative B?

If my friends want to have a pot party, what are the consequences of telling them they're wrong? Of simply not going? Of making an excuse for not going? Of trying to talk them into something different? Choosing among such consequences is difficult, even for the most intelligent child. The adolescent's growth from concrete to abstract thinking or from a physiological moodiness to an adult sense of humor requires the vigilance and loving intervention of parents.

We must be alert to circumstances in their lives and use that awareness to pose hypothetical issues to them at the dinner table or in the car. Kids enjoy intellectual as well as physical activity, especially if the issues being discussed don't affect them directly. General discussions, then, give kids the practice they need to learn the process of moral reflection. Such discussions also provide opportunities for parents to introduce and emphasize the values that are important in their own lives.

Good questions are better than good answers. In this regard, parents must lead children toward good decisions by asking the right questions. They must avoid pushing kids in certain directions by giving what parents consider to be the right answers. You as the parent own the decisions if you make them. We want the kids to own the decisions, so help them decide by asking the kinds of questions that provoke thought. Above all, we must allow them to realize the consequences of their own decisions.

Shared Responsibility

It's important to all good coaches that athletes understand a very important aspect of team membership. It's *their* team. The coaches may seem to have primary responsibility for the operation of the team, but the players determine success or failure, especially during competition.

Youngsters will never share responsibility with their parents or, for that matter, learn the value of moral reflection, if parents make all the decisions. And one of those decisions we are often inclined to make is to bail kids out when they make bad choices. If Chelsea spends her entire school-wardrobe budget on a pair of designer jeans and sweatshirt, sooner or later she's going to recognize that she needs more clothes. How many parents would take Chelsea back to the store, buy her more clothes, and tell her they hoped she learned a lesson from all this. You bet she did. She learned that mom will bail her out every time she makes a bad decision.

There's another very important lesson about family membership that we as parents have to teach our children. Just as athletes must understand that it's their team, kids must realize that it's *their* family. The actual behaviors that make the family a success or a failure rest in large measure with the kids. The decisions they make about school clothes, friends, homework, weekend activities, good deeds, and household chores reflect on the entire family. They also determine how well the family functions. This means that each of us has a job to do.

Years ago, when visiting my in-laws, all three of our girls were eating lunch in the dining room. Kathleen, our oldest, was only three and a half; Carrie was just two and a half. Peggy, not quite a year old, spilled her soup on the floor. Grandma noticed it from the living room and was preparing to go clean it up, when she heard Kathleen say to Carrie, "OK, let's clean it up. She's our baby." My mother-in-law couldn't wait to race outside to tell us the story.

Not much has changed over the years. Kathleen is still the big sister, still laying down an occasional dictum for her sisters but generous to a fault. She is the godmother to both her nephews and has embraced her role as family member with such zeal that she now tells her mom and dad what to do. And we listen. We've discovered that our roles are changing, too.

* * * * * * *

The key to using the reflecting technique is to guide the child through the process of reflecting, judging, deciding, and being responsible. Only by learning the process of moral and ethical reflection will children learn to make good decisions. In addition, moral reflection provides them the opportunity to make such decisions before the actual behavior is required. This enables them to develop an arsenal of well thought out behaviors they can draw on when circumstances require them.

Dialogue - Reflecting

COACH TO PLAYER

Coach: That will *not* happen again, and you know what I'm talking about. You're too strong a person for that.

Player: But he hit me first, and he was foul-mouthing everyone during the whole game.

Coach: So he had a big mouth, hit you, and you hit him back. Is that about it? (Clarify the situation)

Player: Yes. He was a jerk.

Coach: But you were the one who got kicked out of the game.

Player: I can't help if the ref didn't see him hit me first.

Coach: Oh, yes, you can, and you *will* help it from now on. Think for a minute right now and tell me a few other things you might have done. (Begin the process of reflection)

Player: I guess I coulda just pushed him—or just called him a clown. Or I coulda got him after the game.

Coach: What else could you have done? (Push for more alternatives)

Player: I coulda gone nose-to-nose with him and smiled.

Coach: What else? (Be careful not to judge alternatives)

Player: OK, I coulda walked away.

Coach: All right (Still no judging)—keeping in mind that you and I should put forth our absolute best effort during every game, which of those alternatives you just named is the best one? (Provide a standard for judging)

Player: You mean what would I *like* to do?

Coach:	No, hot shot, which one *should* you do to help the team? (Re-emphasize the standard and push for a decision)
Player:	Well, if you put it that way, I guess I should just walk away.
Coach:	OK, think about this, too. What's the toughest thing to do: lose your temper and strike back or control yourself, turn your back, and walk away?
Player:	Walking away.
Coach:	Then the next time it happens, show how really tough you are and walk away. You'll be making a recommitment to your team, too. You're a whole lot more valuable on the field than on the bench.
Player:	OK . . . OK . . . I'll try.
Coach:	No, you won't. You'll *do* it! Tom, we have a shared responsibility for this team, so if you fight again, *I'll* yank you, and you'll sit out the *next* game! The same is true if anything *ever* happens after a game. (Emphasize responsibility for decision)
Player:	OK, OK, message received.
Coach:	Good, let's go to practice.

PARENT TO CHILD

Parent:	What do you mean, you don't want to go to Gramma's, Kathy?
Child:	She yells at me all the time. I can't believe how grumpy she is. Mom, I really don't want to go.
Parent:	Well, she has become a little short-tempered lately. I can see where that might be upsetting to you, but she does love you, you know? (Clarify the situation)
Child:	It sure is hard to tell.

Parent:	Yes, I guess it is sometimes, but that doesn't change the fact that she *does* love you. You love her, too, right?
Child:	Sure I do; I just don't want to be around her.
Parent:	OK, then let's talk about some things you might do to feel more comfortable. (Begin the process of reflection)
Child:	I already know; I just won't go over there.
Parent:	What else might you do? (Push for more alternatives)
Child:	Well, I could go and play outside all day, or I could go and watch TV in the basement the whole time.
Parent:	Can you think of anything else? (Be careful not to judge alternatives)
Child:	(Laughing) Yeah, I could tell Gramma to knock it off!
Parent:	OK, let's talk about that one some more. In other words, maybe you can confront Gramma?
Child:	What? I can't *confront* Gramma!
Parent:	Maybe you can. What about those "I" and "me" statements we were talking about the other day?
Child:	You mean "That makes me feel bad," "I don't know how to respond to that"— that kind of stuff?
Parent:	Yes. Can you tell Gramma when she gets grumpy that it makes you feel bad? That it hurts your feelings?
Child:	I don't know, Mom. That's kinda tough.
Parent:	But you love Gramma, and we both know she loves you. Maybe it will work. (Provide a standard for judging and deciding)
Child:	Well, I don't know. . . .

Parent: Nobody said it would be easy, honey, but sometimes the toughest thing is the best thing. Do you want to try it? You can even think about your exact response beforehand. (Push a little harder for a decision)

Child: OK, but you help me with what I should say.

Parent: I will, and we'll both watch for the right time to do it. We'll make eye contact. You can do this; I know you can. It's just another way of showing how much you love Gramma. (Emphasize responsibility for decision)

Let's Wrap It Up

The primary discussion in this chapter emphasized the importance of unconditional love. Unconditional love will help Kathy confront Gramma, and it will help Gramma change her behavior toward her granddaughter. We have to believe that. Even during the most hopeless moments, we can never doubt the power of love. Loving our children creates consciences in them, and loved children use them. This chapter explained how:

Unconditional love leads to . . .
>Seeing oneself in the eyes of the one who loves you, which leads to . . .
>>Self-criticism and self-control, which leads to . . .
>>>Humility.

Without humility, there is no humanity, and with no humanity, there is no conscience. It was pride that caused the angels to fall from heaven, and it is humility that helps you, me, and our kids get in. We all have to learn to take ourselves less seriously, especially our children. When they realize the focus is off them, all forms of self-gratification become less important: winning, buying, wanting, cheating, lying, drinking, and all those other bad "ing" words that obscure genuine happiness.

Then, when kids lose that tight-fisted grip on "things" and learn the process of reflection, the good "ing" words—caring, sharing, giving, and loving—become their daily focus, and they discover real happiness, the kind that fulfills and completes them. That's why it's important for parents to teach the processes of reflecting, judging, deciding, and being responsible. The earlier kids learn them, the more they will use them when moral and ethical decisions have to be made.

Such reflection is the process by which the child's conscience renews and fortifies itself. A coach can't expect her team to be at its best if her athletes are unable to reflect, judge, and decide during competition. And she can't expect them to really invest themselves in team goals and activities if they don't feel responsible for performance and outcomes. Children must learn the same things as family members. Coaches require reflection and responsibility of their athletes during practice and competition; parents require it of their children at home, in school, and in the community.

Good coaches and parents love children unconditionally so that they learn to love themselves, to trust their own hearts, to believe in the purity of their inner selves. Certainly, they must love their families and believe in their coaches and parents, but every time moral and ethical behavior is needed, they must look to their own consciences. They must look inside themselves and awaken that good person within and listen to its inner voice.

7

COMPETITION
More Than Merely Winning

The desire to win may not be all-consuming for every American, but it's right up there near the top of our national priorities. Beating the other guy is a motivation for people in every corner of this country, from freeways to corporate boardrooms. It's been the goal of sports long before 1869, when fifty students from Princeton and Rutgers layered their clothing for protection before squaring off on the Rutgers Common to stage America's first football game.

Competition even prompted other Ivy League schools not many years later to hire "ringers," itinerant athletes who played for the highest bidder on alternate weekends to win "the big game" for good old Siwash. Coaches even donned the school's colors to beat the other guy. Amos Alonzo Stagg, a former All-American end for Yale and the first head coach at the University of Chicago at the age of twenty-eight, took the field more than a few times to help chalk up another victory for the maroon and yellow.

Only a few years after America's first college football game, beating the other guy became so important that "mass formations" like the Flying Wedge were created. Eventually, they resulted in thirty-three deaths and 246 debilitating injuries and prompted President Theodore Roosevelt in 1906 to tell the "Big Three"—Harvard, Yale, and Princeton—to clean up their act, or he would ban football. Interestingly, while college students were killing each other on the football field and key political figures were condemning their wanton violence, prominent sports writers like Caspar Whitney were singing the praises of "gentlemanly amateurism."

It was a term that had gained favor in England and was fast becoming America's standard for all forms of competition. Whitney's use of the term was in every sense consistent with the class-conscious attitudes that were created in England and eventually flourished in America. In other words, reference to the word "gentleman" had less to do with behavior than with social class. Specifically, he wrote, "The laboring class are all right in their way; let them go their way in peace and have their sport in whatsoever manner best suits their inclinations. . . . Let us have our sport among the more refined elements."

Whitney was only proclaiming the prevailing opinion of the time. Just a few years earlier, London's *Sporting Gazette* asserted that lower class people must recognize ". . . that the facts of their being well-conducted and never having run for money— are not sufficient to make a man a gentleman as well as an amateur." In fact, the London Rowing Association defined a professional as anyone who was a "mechanic, artisan, or laborer." In essence, working class people, by definition, were professionals and were excluded from all forms of "gentlemanly competition."

At its core, therefore, normally little more than a biological urge, winning—at least at the turn of the twentieth century— also had a veneer of social prejudice. That's perhaps the biggest reason why my grandfather, Jim Thorpe, lost his Olympic medals in 1913. He may have been a lot of things, but "refined" he wasn't. By his own admission, he was a "simple Indian school boy" who may have had prodigious athletic ability but who failed the test of being a "gentleman as well as an amateur."

Winning. It's evident, then, that people want to win for a variety of reasons. For turn-of-the-century elitists, it was yet another way to distinguish themselves from the lower classes. For professional athletes, winning meant money, but it also offered a red-necked reaction to the elitism of "gentlemanly amateurism." Ty Cobb climbed into the stands more than once to pound hecklers, and Jim Thorpe's Oorang Indians, the smallest franchise in NFL history, were often frisked for guns and knives before being allowed off trains in early NFL towns.

The situation has not improved much today. According to the National Football League's Players' Association, before the introduction of Proposition 48, as many as two-thirds of college football players failed to graduate from college. And the graduation rates of college basketball players had been as low as twenty-seven percent. Not too many years ago, one of the teams in the NCAA's Final Four had not graduated a black player in more than a decade. Almost every player on the team was black.

So what is it about this phenomenon of winning that makes us so crazy? The answer is simple. Like everything else, when it becomes our exclusive focus, our sole motivation, we're capable of some mighty silly things. In other words, when winning at all costs becomes our most important goal, we lose sight of what's important. We also tend to confuse winning with competition, and competition gets a bad name. Let's put things in perspective.

Why Competition?

In a society shocked daily by the infidelity of government officials, the self-indulgence of professional athletes, and the plain old inconsideration of the guy in the next car, people begin to think warm thoughts about the word "cooperation." "Cooperation" is now at the core of instructional techniques, character education programs in school, and family values at home. "Competition," on the other hand, is getting hit pretty hard by parents and teachers and, for that matter, by anyone who has had a bellyful of chest bumping, trash talking, and gratuitous violence in all forms of sports.

In spite of all the media hype to the contrary, athletic competition is not all bad. I joined forces during my thirty-two-year career with legions of other coaches—in a variety of sports—to develop teamwork, character, and commitment in young athletes. I'm proud and happy that I was responsible for conditioning young bodies, shaping minds, creating character, and making a lot of friends in the process.

I realize, however, that fair-minded fans can't disregard the abuses that provoke sports-page headlines and that upset growing numbers of parents who now question the value of organized sports programs. Consider this example. I was asked a while back by a school system outside Chicago to help a group of coaches, athletes, parents, and others in the community evaluate their athletic program.

The school's administration was concerned that one group of parents wanted the athletic department to offer little more than an intramural program. These parents wanted every child in the school to have an equal chance to participate in a pressure-free sports program. The other group wanted highly competitive teams that consistently vied for state championships. The school's athletic director wanted me to help both groups explore the issues and reach consensus about what they valued in sports. The meetings were productive and very interesting.

The group that favored intramurals soon acknowledged that even late afternoon pick-up games on the sandlot are as competitive as state playoffs. The desire to beat the other guy affects kids as well as adults. Eventually, they also realized that their real concerns were with the win-at-all-costs philosophies of some coaches in organized sports programs. They also resented the growing national emphasis on the athlete in "student-athlete." Once both groups understood these concerns, they discovered that their values regarding athletic competition were quite similar.

They discovered that cooperation and competition are not opposites, that both are good for youngsters. Our children learn self-control by competing *as well as* by cooperating with others. There is no denying that competition is firmly embedded in our culture. Notions of what motivates people have given us everything from merit pay at work to class rank in school. Why is it, then, that as a society, we embrace competition as a motivational practice, yet denounce it as a developmental influence on our children?

Cooperate to Compete

Thirty-two years of coaching helped me to appreciate the value of competition. Many of us confuse winning with competition. We forget that any competition free of an all-consuming desire to win is fun. Learning sociology without the pressure to get an A is fun. Playing field hockey without the need to be All-Conference is fun. That's why kids engage in sports in the first place. They want to have fun, and—if they're lucky—they will. Coaches and parents, therefore, are wise to heed the advice of baseball great Willie Stargell: "Nobody ever said, 'Work ball!' They say, 'Play ball!' To me, that means having fun."

HOW COACHES TEACH THE VALUE OF COMPETITION:

The Lessons of Winning

Good coaches see more in competition than *merely* winning. They realize, for example, that athletes and coaches who seek victory at all costs diminish their own sense of accomplishment. Consider injury to a gifted opponent. Good coaches realize that when opponents are not at their best, their own team suffers. If we compete not just to win but to perfect ourselves in the pursuit of victory, then the loss of a worthy opponent hurts us as well as the opposing team. We are no longer pushed to play our best, and the ultimate victory is diminished. Winning is only one result of competition. More important are the personal commitment, self-sacrifice, and willingness to stand toe-to-toe with a tough challenge. To me and to a lot of coaches and athletes, *that's* fun.

The Lessons of Losing

Competition also involves losing. Fortunately, much can be learned from it. It is a moment of disappointment that teems with opportunities for understanding and improvement. Children who learn its lessons, as severe as they may be, discover how to win, and, invariably, they do win. They become winners not only on the field or in the gymnasium but at home, at work, and in school. The willingness to persist is itself a victory, and persistence is impossible without a worthy challenge. Losing is never final. It can and should be a spur to persist toward the goal, whatever that goal may be.

Beyond Winning

Obviously, then, good coaches understand that the outcome of a game is secondary to the commitment each player must make to win it. One part of that commitment involves the cooperation that unites individual players into a team. Good coaches know that athletes who make such commitments and who learn such cooperation develop the self-control that wins games. More important, the athletes learn to "refuse to lose" in all walks of life, particularly in those areas that promote pride and self-worth. Only competition teaches such lessons.

A Little Self-Evaluation Goes a Long Way

To push kids beyond winning, they need the ability and the inclination to review their own behavior and critically evaluate it. Every Monday following a game, our players were expected to use a free period during the school day to watch the game tape and use a form we provided to observe and evaluate their own performance. On the form, we asked them to identify skills they had to work on, even to suggest drills that we might use during practice that week. We would collect all the forms at the end of the day and integrate them into that week's practice schedule. We were constantly amazed at how hard the kids worked when they helped identify the drills.

HOW PARENTS TEACH THE VALUE OF COMPETITION:

Get Kids to Be Team Players

Kids learn self-control when they cooperate with others and put some of their personal needs on hold in order to achieve group needs. The question is, how important to them are these group needs? It's really a question of comparison. If I'm standing on the edge of a curb, balance is not a critical issue to me. If I'm on the edge of a cliff, balance assumes new meaning for me.

Kids are more motivated to work hard and learn the values of competition if the group need is important enough. They want to win games, springboard competitions, and 100-meter sprints. When they discover that achieving the group need also helps them achieve their personal need, cooperation becomes desirable. This is just another example of how cooperation and competition complement each other.

Emphasize teamwork. Parents, don't tell junior to cooperate because that's what you want; help him want it, too. If you want your child to learn the lessons of competition, emphasize "teamness" in the family. The notion that we're all in this together is critical. Your family is a team with common needs and goals. Spend time together—play together, cry together, laugh together, plan together, and yes, eat together, and talk together. Sounds hackneyed? Of course it does—only because it's been true for so long.

Like it or not, our families are in competition with a whole range of forces that are conspiring against our most important values. Like coaches, we must expect our children to have the personal commitment, self-sacrifice, and willingness to stand toe-to-toe with one of the toughest challenges ever to face the family. Never before in our history have the media and other forms of technology posed such a significant threat to our values. We're in a real battle, and parents must be constantly alert for opportunities to reinforce what is important to the family.

Put Competition in Perspective

Value, therefore, the effort that goes into a win, not the win itself. Value the time spent on study, not the grade itself. Value the willingness to take challenging courses, not the class rank itself. Value the child's willingness to laugh, not the silly joke itself. When you and your children value effort and a simple love of life, the children learn self-control. They develop the discipline it takes to keep making the effort.

Hard work really is its own reward. The real value of competition, then, is found in the effort, not the result. Like cooperation, competition develops self-control, especially when children compete with themselves. It's a competition they can win virtually every time. Every time I work harder, study more, or enjoy a good laugh, I win. Kids can't always get an A or score the winning goal, but they can always keep working hard. When they do, they develop and reveal more character.

Refuse to Quit

Remember Rachel and her coach, Mrs. Dietrich? Mrs. Dietrich always acknowledged superior performance, but, more important, she recognized superior effort. She knew that every player on her team, regardless of her athletic limitations, was capable of such effort. And she knew that if everyone made this effort—if they consistently refused to quit—the team would win its share of games. More important, they would exhibit the winning attitude that resulted in continuing effort, and nothing is more valuable to youngsters later in life.

Share the Moment

Share the moment—whether cooperative or competitive—with your child. Coaches get excited when young athletes learn new skills, put forth extra effort, or help a teammate. Many pat deserving athletes on the back or give them hugs. An excited response from parents shapes children's behavior. It is reinforcing to them. Such reinforcement provides recognition and influences children to repeat the behaviors, in effect, to develop character.

Remember, they'll do what is rewarding, not what gets rewarded. Certainly, we don't want to give children five dollars every time they help us. That could get pretty expensive, and we also know that external rewards influence children very little. We want them to feel good about doing something positive. If the act is intrinsically reward*ing*—rather than extrinsically reward*ed*—it gets repeated. Our job as parents is to help our kids understand the value of helping others and the satisfaction of a job well done.

On the other hand, just because you're involved with your children, don't expect them to do backflips to help you do the laundry. Kids are still pretty self-focused. They'll pick fun over work most of the time. So will you and I. But at least you and I have learned that if our jobs are intrinsically rewarding, we like them. Kids learn similar lessons, if we promote the right things.

Promote a Little Self-Criticism

One of the things to promote is the effectiveness of their performance. Your daughter can't watch a game tape of how well she mows the lawn, but she can evaluate her own performance by looking at the lawn when she finishes the job. Your son can't watch a tape of how well he paints the front fence, but he can look it over when he's done. It always seems easier for parents to point out the missed spots, but it doesn't teach children the value of self-criticism. Engage them in a little self-competition. Help them evaluate their own performance and make necessary changes.

But let's not be too critical. How many times have you and I been convinced we couldn't do something—until we did it? Because this has happened so often to me, I learned a long time ago to accept my limitations reluctantly. Kids must feel the same way. Most coaches have known young athletes who were either too slow or too small, sometimes both. They've also learned to suspend judgment because, with time, many of these kids have become bigger and faster. The child who accepts his limitations at an early age never learns to overcome them.

Consider the child who may seem intellectually slow. Einstein didn't talk until he was three or four years old. We must not forget that normal developmental growth can transform apparent limitations into nothing more than bumps on the road. This is not to say, however, that grown children shouldn't gain a knowledge of themselves. Self-knowledge identifies our strengths and limitations and leads to opportunities to capitalize on the strengths and to compensate for the limitations. The following sample dialogue suggests ways to help children develop such self-knowledge.

* * * * * * *

Looking inside is a technique that focuses more on questions than on answers. It emphasizes open-ended questions, the kind that can't be answered with a simple yes or no. Looking inside helps the child explore issues; it doesn't seek information or simple agreement. That's why it emphasizes "what," "where," and "how" questions, rarely "why" questions. When you help children look inside, you're not asking them to justify their behavior or explain a certain decision. You're asking them to look deep inside and to explore areas that they never imagined, areas that lead to even further exploration and, hopefully, sudden insight.

Dialogue - Looking Inside

COACH TO PLAYER

Player: I need your help. I have five colleges that want me to play next year. Two are Division 3 and three are Division 2. But I only like two of them; one D2 and one D3.

Coach: OK, what's the problem?

Player: I can get a partial scholarship at the D2 school, nothing at the D3.

Coach: First question: Can your parents afford to send you to college?

Player: Yeah, the money's been set aside for a long time.

Coach: Good for them. Next question: What has to happen within the next half hour to help you make a decision? (First "what" question to provoke exploration. Be ready. "Looking inside" questions stop kids in their tracks and often are followed by complete silence.)

Player: Wow. . . . I don't know. . . . I guess I need information.

Coach: What else do you need? (Another "what" question to provoke even more exploration)

Player: Well, . . . I guess I need you to tell me what to do!

Coach: Ha, forget that one, Jason. This is your decision. What else?

Player: I guess I need good reasons for a final decision.

Coach: OK, then let me ask you this question: Picture yourself in a job five to ten years from now. What are you doing? And what does your future self tell you to do now to get there?

Player: The first part's easy. I'm just about to become a partner in a New York law firm.

Coach:	Hey, good! I'll have free legal advice! Now—what's your future self telling you?
Player:	Well. . . . He's saying get the best preparation you can get—and get into a good law school.
Coach:	OK, what will it take to make that happen? (Another "what" question)
Player:	And the light goes on! It'll take the D3 school; it's a much better school.
Coach:	Yes, it is. (Agree with the player only after he's explored the issue)
Player:	But I'd get a scholarship at the D2 school.
Coach:	So what? (This is sometimes the most provocative "looking inside" question of all)
Player:	Well, I don't know. I just like the idea of having a scholarship.
Coach:	Yeah, I can understand that, but what will that get you compared to what your future self is telling you? (Another "what" question)
Player:	Yeah, no comparison, really, huh?
Coach:	I don't know; what do you think? (Final "what" question)
Player:	Thanks, Coach; I think I know what I'm gonna do.

PARENT TO CHILD

Child:	I think I want to run for vice president of Student Council again, but I'm not sure.
Parent:	Well, how do you *feel* about it? (Start the exploration with a consideration of emotions)
Child:	Well, deep inside I want to try, but I ran last year and lost, so I'm not sure.
Parent:	What has to happen to make you sure? (Tough question but essential for the child to consider)

Child:	Gee, I don't know. (Parent should not dive in now; give the child time to think. That's when the best exploration takes place.) I guess I have to stop worrying about losing.
Parent:	Then let's put it this way, honey. What would you do if you weren't worrying about losing? (Excellent "what" question. This kind of question helps open the door for lots of kids.)
Child:	Wow. I guess I'd run.
Parent:	Let's put it this way—if you could wipe the slate clean from last year, what would you do?
Child:	I'd run.
Parent:	Then, what's stopping you? (Good looking inside question. It forces a hard look at oneself.)
Child:	Well. . . . I guess just this crazy fear.
Parent:	What are you going to do about it? (Final "what" question)
Child:	Oh, what the heck. Let's go for it.
Parent:	Good luck, honey. What can I do to help?
Child:	I'm not sure; I'll let you know. Thanks, Mom.

Keep in mind that these are tough questions for lots of kids. Some children are more than a little queasy about plumbing the depths of their psyches. They're not altogether sure what they're going to find there. But when all is said and done, when the process is complete, they're usually very happy with themselves. It's almost as if they've climbed a very steep hill and now find themselves in a wonderful position to enjoy the view.

Helping Kids Compete

As soon as kids walk out the front door, they bump into competition. It's everywhere. They jockey for position getting on the school bus, contend for a good class rank, run for class elections, and try out for sports teams. Even at home, they struggle for supremacy of the checkerboard, compete for their parents' attention, and wage basketball battles on the driveway. Kids can't escape competition, nor should they. Our job is to make sure they enter each competition with the confidence to try their hardest, to win with humility, and to lose with dignity, and a willingness to learn from the experience.

Add to the competition the expectations we have of our children. Whether coaches or parents, we feel that we have a good understanding of their strengths and weaknesses. We expect them to do well in certain situations and not so well in others. Those of us who have been through the experience of raising children have learned the effect our expectations have on them, so we share a bit of advice: Be careful.

The reality of the self-fulfilling prophecy looms large in families, as well as athletic teams. What we expect of our children and how we relate to them has a profound influence on what they will be, much more profound than any of us realizes. These influences can be very subtle, so parents and coaches must be constantly alert to their expectations and, more important, *how* they impose them on kids.

Expectations Are Not Cast in Bronze

Years of educational research point out consistently that many of us, teachers especially, develop expectations of kids based on their race, gender, socioeconomic condition, clothing, and even physical appearance. Obviously, the expectations of parents are affected differently. Gender bias may sometimes be an issue with parents; it sneaks into some of the best families. But the other factors rarely influence parents.

Coaches are not interested in socioeconomic status, race, or appearance. Most coaches are interested primarily in one thing—performance. Does the youngster have the skills and the talent to play this game well? Is she going to help the team? Coaches get such information from two primary sources: other coaches and/or simple observation. How they handle the information depends on their competence and maturity, as well as the accuracy of the information.

Some coaches will develop expectations of certain kids and, later, alter their opinions based on continued observation. In other words, if a poorly performing athlete suddenly performs consistently well, the coach will raise his expectations of the youngster. On the other hand, less effective coaches attribute the athlete's sudden improvement to luck and refuse to change their expectations. Obviously, *good* coaches are flexible and change their earlier expectations based on the athlete's improved performance.

Expectations = Behavior
This flexibility is critical to the success of the athlete, as well as to the total athletic program. Good coaches understand that their expectations alone don't create self-fulfilling prophecies. This is a very important point. What I *expect* of Tom as he struggles to master his passing motion is only a small part of how successful Tom will be. The issue is, will I allow my expectations of Tom to influence the amount of *practice and instruction* I give him? Will I allow my expectations to determine how well I relate to him? The level of instruction is the key factor.

Remember Rachel? She was affected the same way. If her coach had been convinced that Rachel was too small to play basketball and, on that basis, had failed to give her practice time or consistent instruction, Rachel would not have improved. At that point, the coach's expectations would have been reinforced, and she would have continued to overlook Rachel. So what do good coaches do? They remain flexible and change their expectations of young athletes and, above all, work hard to provide instruction, practice, and corrective feedback to *all* players, some of whom, like Rachel, blossom into full-blown stars. Rachel would not have stood a chance if her coach didn't help her. And if she didn't provide that help and Rachel failed to progress, she would have created a self-fulfilling prophecy—not just by what the coach expected but by what she failed to provide Rachel.

Self-Fulfilling Prophecies Can Be Vicious Circles

What is especially bad is that the process is cyclical. When I expect poor performance, I usually fail to give instruction. Then, when the athlete fails to improve, I continue to expect poor performance. What's especially bad is that when the athlete fails to perform well, I feel pretty smart! I knew he couldn't do it—and he didn't. This is yet another example of the need for all of us to take an occasional look in the mirror to determine if we are doing what we should be doing to help our kids grow. Is it that the child simply can't do it, or am *I* falling down on the job?

Good coaches break this cycle by expecting *every* athlete to improve, no matter what his or her skill level. If this expectation is communicated consistently and corrective instruction is provided for all athletes, every child will improve. Some coaches will even find the time to stay after practice with low-performing athletes to give them the instruction they need to meet the coach's expectations that they will improve.

I had a middle linebacker one year who was 5′8″ tall and weighed about 155 pounds. His name was Fred, and even as I write this, I can't believe how small he was. But he was an explosive kid—the body of a bullet, the impact and instincts of a guided missile. In practice, he was on the bottom of every pile; so often, in fact, that we asked ourselves: "How can we keep this kid out of a game?" So, late in the second quarter of our first game, we put him in. He was our starting middle linebacker for the rest of the year.

Never sell a child short, any child. They are amazing creatures.

Go Easy on Your Expectations

Parental expectations are different from those of teachers and coaches. Although teachers and coaches want kids to compete successfully and be happy, their wishes don't compare to what parents want for their kids. Babies born to most families are success stories waiting to happen, living proof of the perfectibility of the human race. As children grow, they look to the family for the continuing expression of this warmth and devotion, but the family also begins to impose expectations on them.

Most often, these expectations are realistic, but sometimes they are downright unreasonable. Consider the case of a mother who wanted her family doctor to prescribe human growth hormone for her son. She wanted him to be taller so he would get a scholarship to college. She really didn't care about the lessons of competition. Like so many unprincipled coaches and self-focused kids, all she cared about was the status that came with the scholarship.

At the other extreme, some parents expect their children to follow in their footsteps, to accomplish the same things they did. An acquaintance of mine, a former college athlete, expected his son to follow in his footsteps. When all was said and done, not only did the child refuse to play football, but he and his dad never really became good friends. Unreasonable expectations will do that. It happens elsewhere, too. Formerly successful students want straight As from their kids. Good businessmen want the kids in the family business, or in the same profession, and so it goes.

Certainly, these expectations are not all bad. *Usually*, however, extreme expectations place unfair demands on kids, especially when parents push too hard. Let's face it, anything to an extreme is potentially destructive, so parents are well-advised to impose reasonable expectations on their kids and to give them all the support they need to achieve them. Like good coaches, we must also be flexible, adjusting expectations as our kids grow.

Relationships Are Still Most Important

Again like good coaches, we must realize that our expectations alone don't create self-fulfilling prophecies. The behavior created by these expectations is the key. If Mike struggles with math, he'll lose the battle if we fail to help him. We may be convinced that he has lousy math ability, but we can't let that stop us from helping him. With such help, we may be in for a big surprise. Working with kids involves one pleasant surprise after another. Well, sometimes they're not so pleasant—but they're always surprises.

On the other hand, we might like to see Cathy become an All-American forward for Tennessee. Wanting it for her and pushing her into it, however, are two different things. If we push a little too hard, we may turn her off completely, and, at that point, the degree of instruction or practice we provide won't make any difference anyway.

Practice and instruction, then, work best in areas that are relevant for the child. Like it or not, their relevance for you is somewhat less important! A well-motivated child will listen to instruction and work hard in practice, no matter what the activity, whether at home or in school. An unmotivated child probably won't do either, no matter how hard we push. Isn't it intriguing, then, to think that we develop self-fulfilling prophecies by providing too little support and instruction—or too much? Obviously, the safest ground is somewhere in between these two extremes.

Reach Out and Keep Reaching Out

The best way to stay on safe ground is to do what coaches do: expect every child to improve. This has added benefits as well. The more corrective feedback we give kids, the more competent they think they are. Assume that two of your children, one younger than the other, ask you to proofread their homework assignments in English. Both papers are of equal quality, so you congratulate both children for their effort and merit. But you give more corrective feedback to the younger child because you believe that she has more potential as a writer.

Your behavior has affected each child differently. Of the two children, the younger will feel more competent, even though you congratulated them both equally. By giving her corrective feedback, you have unintentionally suggested that she is capable of better work. By giving your older child little or no feedback, you have suggested that he is probably incapable of better work.

Think about it. Intending to compliment both children, you have improved the self-concept of one and slighted the other. Which of the two will be more self-assured when competing for grades in English?

Corrective feedback is so valuable. Writer George Eliot provided one of my favorite quotes: "It is never too late to be what you might have been." Applied to me, the quote suggests that I keep working to be the best person I can be. Applied to my children, it suggests that I work even harder to help them be their best, recognizing all the while that they are capable of far more than even I imagine. Corrective feedback given to both children, therefore, helps them both improve their writing skills and gives each of them an improved sense of competence. And you and I both know that kids who believe in themselves accomplish a great deal in life.

Let's look again at the role of praise. We already have discussed the problem of general praise. It makes kids dependent on the person who gives it and does little to improve performance. General praise also can negatively affect a child's self-concept. As surprising as that sounds, consider this. Kids who receive more praise than the others for the same level of performance usually perceive themselves as having lower ability, and the more effusive the praise, the lower the ability. In addition, effusive praise is more likely to embarrass them.

Conversely, when kids are at the same level of performance, the ones who receive corrective instruction are perceived by others—as well as by themselves—to be more competent and capable of improved performance. This is yet another reason to expect improvement from every child and to give them all corrective feedback. Such feedback not only promotes the child's improved performance but enhances his or her self-concept.

Hold Their Attention

Biased treatment of one child, no matter how subtle, creates other problems as well. Most good coaches learned a long time ago that obviously biased treatment of one player turns off other players. In other words, if I shower an equal measure of specific recognition and corrective feedback only on my star player, other players are going to stop listening to me. It's likely they'll look to other persons (parents, friends, fans) for affirmations of their competence.

If this happens in the family, parents have closed important lines of communication. As important, they have weakened, however incidentally, the opportunity to connect with other children in the family to influence their development and to enhance their self-concepts. So let every child in the family know that you have important but reasonable expectations of them and are willing to give them as much help as they need to meet them.

When You Have to Put the Heat On

For whatever reason, even the best kids will dig in their heels and fight us, sometimes a little, sometimes a lot. When they fight us a lot, it's time to look in the nearest mirror again and ask ourselves what we're doing wrong. But when they fight us a little, that's to be expected. Their path to independence involves a variety of battles at almost every turn. But the inevitability of it doesn't mean we don't respond. All kids need parenting once in a while, just as athletes, no matter how great, need coaching. Without it, they don't compete as well.

They need our involvement to correct the behaviors that interfere with proper performance and the ability to compete. My quarterback needs me to remind him to follow through on his passing motion, just as my child needs me to remind her to follow through on her decision to see her teacher for extra help. There's really not much difference; both result in a better delivery. *That* we provide such correction is not the issue; *how* we provide it is the focus of this section.

For Most Kids, Keep the Stress Low

Opera star Beverly Sills once said, "You may be disappointed when you fail, but you're doomed if you don't try again." Good coaches know that some kids need a great deal of support to learn this lesson. When kids' failures become habits, however, we have to ask ourselves some important questions. Are the tasks beyond their ability? Is something else in their lives interfering with their completion? Am I getting in the way with expectations that may be out of line? Or are they just slacking off?

The first three questions are very important. We don't want interferences preventing our kids from competing successfully. Our job is to get rid of obstacles. And sometimes that involves some tough decisions for us. We may have to face up to possible learning disabilities. We may have to acknowledge some problems at home or in school. Or we may have to look carefully into the mirror and admit if we're expecting too much.

The fourth question is important, too, but it usually involves a different response from us. Kids slack off for as many reasons as there are kids. The first step is to find the reason.

The second step is to do something about it. If it's plain old laziness or an adolescent unwillingness to do homework, chores, or whatever else is expected, the child has to face the consequences. But what are the reasonable consequences of laziness or childish resistance?

Punishment is usually not the answer. That's right. Punishment may change unwanted behaviors, but it also involves more unwanted side effects than spoiled milk. Punishment works for one reason. It arouses fear, usually a fear of failure. Kids fear failure because they know it will provoke a punishment. At that point, competition isn't just a challenge; it's a threat, and their healthy desire to achieve becomes a nagging fear of failure.

This is when kids "choke," when their own anxiety trips them up. Their fear of failure makes them tighter than banjo strings, and they choke on major homework assignments and during ACTs, final exams, and interviews for jobs and college admission. So if you want your kids to fear failure and misunderstand the whole idea of competition, punish them every time they fail. Punish them every time they forget a homework assignment or a chore around the house. Clearly, you don't want that.

Nor do you want your kids to resent you when you punish them. As important, you don't want them to consciously or unconsciously undercut your efforts when you try to accomplish something with or for them. It happens in sports and it happens at home. Kids who resent their coaches unconsciously find ways to lose ball games. And children who resent their parents find ways to forget homework assignments. They do it unconsciously, which makes it even harder to deal with.

Punishment destroys peak performance and prevents kids from competing successfully. That alone tells us that it should never be the first thing we do when kids misbehave or fail.

Let Them Know How They're Doing

The first thing good coaches do to correct failure is give kids objective feedback. Providing feedback focuses the athlete and the coach on what has to be done to compete successfully. It may increase stress for the athlete, but it also increases a focus on the task or activity. When Bill does a lousy job pass blocking in our last game, I'm going to do what I do best— increase his stress level! But I'm going to make sure that he focuses on the right way to pass block and that he hears— loudly and clearly—how well he's doing. This is a reasonable consequence.

And what if I discover in the process that he just doesn't have the strength or the quickness to block bigger opponents? Or that he's having problems with three or four of his team-mates? Or with his parents? I handle those problems first. Or, like John Wooden, I expect him to focus in practice and han-dle these problems later—with my help. But the problems have to be addressed sometime, because I can give Bill feedback about his pass blocking until I'm blue in the face, and he still won't compete successfully until these other issues are handled.

Kids need the same thing. When your youngest forgets once too often to do his math homework, he needs a reason-able consequence. And what is more reasonable than doing math? Tackles pass block; kids do math. They may not like it, and they might even consider it a punishment. And maybe there is a fine line between a punishment and a reasonable con-sequence, but that line becomes more distinct when you and I impose the consequence with the right attitude—gently, kind-ly, but persistently.

And what if you discover in the process that he is really struggling with math and getting more frustrated by the day? What if he's at odds with his math teacher? What if he has a learning disability? What if a bully in class is picking on him? These problems have to be handled first. Let's admit it. Like it or not, his math class involves competition for grades. Any obstacle to successful competition has to be removed. Talk to the math teacher. Find out how class is going. Maybe he needs to be tested. Maybe you need to meet with the teacher. Initially, at least, kids need the benefit of the doubt when they screw up.

I taught educational supervision in a Chicago university for twenty-three years, and one of the most intriguing insights I shared with my students was taught to me by W. Edwards Demming, the world's most gifted organizational consultant.

Demming's appearance suggested a deep-voiced wall of a man, demanding and unforgiving, but his message was gentle. It proposed caring and support—even in the most competitive situations.

Demming asserted frequently that ninety to ninety-five percent of problems in any organization are caused by the organization itself. Even when employees resist or cause problems, managers and leaders must look within the system to find what might be causing their behavior. If they look objectively, they'll find it. If they persist in blaming employees, not only won't they find the problem but they'll cause more problems. Families are the most important organizations in our culture, profound in their impact on kids and subject to the same kinds of organizational issues. Sometimes we must recognize that the problem may be in the family, not the child.

Keep the Pressure Off

The very first thing good businessmen and good coaches do, therefore, when their people aren't competing successfully is ask themselves, "What am I doing to contribute to this problem?" If they're not the problem, the next thing they ask is, "What interferences are getting in the way of this kid's performance?" If there are any, we had better get them out of the way.

Maybe our best advice is to look at punishment differently. During my playing days at Nebraska, I learned quickly that when I and my teammates screwed up in a drill, we would see it again the next day. It might even be tougher, but, in spite of how hard I had to work, I never looked at it as punishment. I didn't like it, but it seemed reasonable to me. I knew that if I was to compete successfully, I would need the skill. So I did it. Kids will respond much the same way to your reasonable consequences.

How *you* behave makes the difference. If your behavior suggests punishment, however, they'll react differently. In fact, your behavior may be the one factor that makes the difference between punishment and reasonable consequences much more than semantic. If you react in anger or if your punishments are arbitrary, that is, if there is no logical connection between the misbehavior and the punishment, your children will fail to focus on their own wrongdoing.

When that happens, they are in danger of joining the misguided many out there who give the appearance of proper behavior—not because they honor character but because they fear punishment. At that point, competition involves cheating or doing whatever is necessary to win. I don't know one good coach who wanted to win under those circumstances. Winning at the expense of integrity is the worst kind of losing.

Keep the Consequences Reasonable—But Keep Them Coming!

Devising reasonable consequences isn't always easy. Often, our anger gets in the way, and we all know that we don't think clearly when our fists are clenched. So the first thing we have to do is control our anger.

Mark Twain once said, "When angry, count to ten; when very angry, swear." Sound like Twain? Not bad advice either, as long as you swear to yourself and keep your mouth shut while doing it. Good coaches know the value of staying cool. Anger is not a very good teacher. Even when we do control our anger, we often discover that a good reasonable consequence can be as uncomfortable for us as it is for the kids. When Bill surrenders the car keys for two weeks, we have to drive him to and from practice. When Molly is grounded from a weekend of party-going, we have to protect ourselves all night from her laser-like "look."

Is "grounding" a reasonable consequence? Yes, it is! When kids are irresponsible, we can't sit comfortably at home while they drive from one potential danger to another. When Bill drives carelessly, we can't let him drive. When Molly drinks at a party, we can't let her go to parties. It's that simple. At such times, just a quick glimpse in the mirror tells us we didn't do anything wrong. Our kids did. That's the time to impose consequences—as many as it takes to change the child's behavior and develop a little character.

Often, one consequence leads to another. One year, one of my daughters was having trouble with social studies. She missed a couple important papers. The teacher even gave us a call. Needless to say, my daughter and I had a little talk. She wasn't having any problems with the class; she just forgot to do the papers. So we all agreed that she should spend at least an hour and a half in her room after dinner to do all her homework, especially her social studies.

A short time later, I called the teacher. Was she getting all her work in? No? She missed one more homework assignment? My daughter, my wife, and I had another talk. My wife and I told her very matter-of-factly—but firmly—that for the next several nights, she would sit in the kitchen and do her homework so we could be available to help her, and to be able to check on her progress. *When* she wanted to do it was up to her. During the first half hour of the first night, she just sat there, arms folded and jaw set. Finally, my wife said, "Oh, as soon as you're done, honey, you can watch TV or call your friends." Pretty soon, she reached for a book and appeared to do all her work.

This went on for five nights. I called the teacher again. He told me that all her work was in and that she actually volunteered some opinions during a recent class discussion. I asked him to call if her work trailed off again. We continued the kitchen routine for one more week, then had another talk. It ended with, "Well, what do you think, kiddo, back to your room for homework?" "You bet!" she answered. "Can we count on everything getting done?" "Yes," she said. Smiles around and off she went to call a friend.

Sometimes the problems are bigger than we think. If your child consistently refuses to accept reasonable consequences, no matter how objectively you try to impose them, and if his or her misbehavior is the rule rather than the exception, you have another kind of problem. Sometimes the frustrating but predictable misbehaviors of a normally developing child give way to the intransigence and hostility of a maladjusted child. At these times, parents need outside help. That's the time to talk to school counselors, social workers and youth officers in the community, or private consultants.

Just be sure to do it. Maladjusted children become maladjusted adults, and in a competitive society such as ours, they find themselves without the educational and emotional tools to realize whatever potential they possess. They are very much a part of a growing tragedy in our society—people who create more Columbines or, less dramatically, who fail at marriage, a career, or the raising of their own children.

* * * * * * *

"Correcting" is a last-resort technique. Although it can incorporate most of the techniques already discussed in this book, it assumes that any previous interactions with kids have been only marginal successful. Although, if your efforts with your kids are anything like mine, a "*marginal* success" is cause for unbridled celebration. Our biblical counterparts killed the fatted calf. My wife and I just sneaked out of the house for a Big Mac and a few self-satisfied smiles.

But even marginal success can be insufficient, so sometimes we have a little "heart to heart" with our kids. That's when "correcting" comes in handy. It is an adult-directed technique that accepts the child's input but has very specific predetermined outcomes. There comes a time in every relationship when one of the two parties has to take a stand. It is not a time for shouting or letting our anger get the best of us, even though that often happens. In fact, because emotions usually run high at these times, our self-control and sound judgment are especially important.

Dialogue - Correcting

COACH TO PLAYER

Coach:	Cindy, that's the third time in two games you blew an easy roller to third base. (Coach identifies the problem)
Player:	Yeah, we talked about it a couple times.
Coach:	(Smiling) We sure did. And you didn't find the time to practice your fielding, did you? (Coach identifies more specifics without being angry)
Player:	Well, I guess I forgot.
Coach:	That's too bad because your lack of practice resulted in another error.
Player:	Yeah, so, we won the game, didn't we?
Coach:	That's not the point, Cindy. If you don't work on your fielding, you might make an error when it *does* cost us a game.
Player:	Yeah, OK, I'll find time to work on grounders.
Coach:	Sounds good. So will I. In fact, you and I both will work on grounders. You'll pick 'em up, and I'll watch you. (Introduce a reasonable consequence, one that provides objective performance feedback)
Player:	What? I don't need that. I'll do it this time. I promise.
Coach:	Yes, you will do it, and here are your three options. You can stay after practice this week, or you can get out to practice early, or we'll meet on the practice field forty-five minutes before our next couple games. (Allow the athlete to choose an alternative but within the coach's parameters)
Player:	Come on, Coach. That's not fair. I'll work harder in practice.
Coach:	Glad to hear about the harder work, but let's talk about fair. You're the coach and I'm the player, and I blow three easy

	grounders and keep forgetting to do anything about it. What do *you* do? (Use reversing technique)
Player:	OK, something's gotta happen, but isn't there any other way?
Coach:	Nope. When do we get together?
Player:	OK, I'll get out to practice early tomorrow.
Coach:	No, you'll get out to practice early for the next three days—a half hour early—and I'll be here waiting for you. (Promote accountability)
Player:	OK. OK.
Coach:	(Smiling) See you tomorrow.

Notice that the coach said nothing about replacing the player if she keeps making errors. Such a threat would have a negative impact on her performance. As indicated several times in this book, the threat of punishment promotes a fear of failure, and nothing is more harmful to peak performance.

PARENT TO CHILD

Parent:	How'd it go at practice?
Child:	Pretty good, but I have to get to practice early for the next three days to work on grounders with Coach.
Parent:	Problems?
Child:	Yeah, I made three errors in the last two games.
Parent:	Yes, I noticed. Well, have fun! You know, you may not be having a really good day! Now *I* have to talk with you.
Child:	Why? Now what?
Parent:	I noticed your room this afternoon. I think every piece of clothing you own is on the floor. (Parent identifies the problem)

Child:	Come on, Dad, I've really been busy lately.
Parent:	So have I, but my suits and ties aren't all over my floor.
Child:	OK, I'll keep it clean.
Parent:	Whoa. How many times have I heard that one? Yes, you will keep it clean, and I'll watch you. (Introduce a reasonable alternative, one that promotes objective performance feedback)
Child:	What? This really *is* deja vu all over again! Did you talk to Coach?
Parent:	Nope, I didn't talk to your coach, but I sure like her style. Here's what you can do. You can clean your room before church on Sunday, or you can do it sometime on Saturday. (Allow the child to choose an alternative but within the parent's parameters)
Child:	I've got a game on Saturday! This isn't fair.
Parent:	OK, let's talk about fair. I'm you and you're me. You spend hundreds of dollars on my clothes every year, and I walk on them more than I wear them. (Use reversing technique)
Child:	OK, OK! Man, you guys really *are* on the same wavelength!
Parent:	Good! What's your decision?
Child:	Before church on Sunday.
Parent:	Sounds good, but it will be before church the next three Sundays, and your old man will be right there with you. Hopefully, after that, you'll keep your room clean, and in between Sundays, you won't have your clothes all over the floor. Or guess what? You and I will have another talk. (Promote accountability)

| Child: | Fine. Fine. Geez, what a day! |
| Parent: | Yeah, you've had better ones, haven't you! |

Notice that dad didn't get angry, but he remained firm throughout the entire talk. Nor did he threaten Cindy that if the problem continued, she would have to buy her own clothes. That might come later. For now, he didn't want to confuse the issue with possible negative comments. Peak performance applies to cleaning rooms, too!

What jumps out at most parents when I discuss this dialoguing technique is that both the coach and the dad took on more work, too. They had to be with Cindy during the consequences. Well, as the Duke said in one of his movies, "Goes with the badge!" That kind of thing happens when we decide to be good parents. The good thing is, it's time well spent. Cindy will learn something. She may need an occasional reminder in the future, but the experience didn't involve any yelling, and it will save us a lot of time in the future.

I learned a simple fact with my own children. The more I yelled, the more I *had* to yell. Getting angry and losing my temper didn't seem to resolve problems. In fact, it created more than a few. The same was true in coaching. The more I yelled, the less the kids listened to me. The more reasonable I was, the more reasonable they were. It was as simple as that. Then, on those rare occasions when I did raise my voice—and I always knew why I was doing it—they *really* listened. When we get angry, the emotions take over and the mind goes blank. And I learned a long time ago that the mind is like a TV set. When it goes blank, it's always a good idea to turn off the sound.

Let's Wrap It Up

This chapter has praised competition. In the best of circumstances, it introduces kids to all the values we've discussed in this book, whether the kids are competing or just watching. Consider George Will's comment: "Sports serve society by providing vivid examples of excellence." Even Supreme Court Chief Justice Earl Warren once said, "I always turn to the sports page first. The sports page records people's accomplishments; the front page has nothing but man's failures."

It's no wonder that kids make role models of the most obvious examples of excellence in our society. Fortunately, they also imitate the great role models sitting around the dinner table, standing in front of them in class, or leading calisthenics during practice. The world is full of common people who do uncommon things—without receiving fanfare or making millions of dollars. Witness the thousands of people in New York City who transformed the tragedy at the World Trade Center into a showcase of courage and love. They are marvelous role models.

You don't have to be a great theologian or a quantum scientist to know that if we could boil down beauty, truth, justice, wisdom, and all the other absolutes we seek in life to just one thing, it would be love. Love is the most powerful force on earth. The author George Sand once said, "There is only one happiness in life—to love and to be loved." Her quote suggests that love is a verb, not a noun. In other words, it is one thing to feel love for someone, another to express it. Let us express love, and keep expressing it, in everything we do with our children.

Ten Common Myths About Parenting

Some coaches and most parents routinely accept a few popular beliefs about raising and working with kids. Like all myths, they have been sanctioned by time but usually fall short of being accurate. In fact, many of these myths do more harm than good. They are dispelled throughout this book.

Myth #1—Like coaches, parents have to be good motivators. Children require a lot of external motivation.

Myth #2—Good parents realize that kids also need lots of praise if they are to perform well.

Myth #3—Parents must always extend themselves for their children. It is a sure sign of love.

Myth #4—Parents must be sure to constantly reward positive behavior. Such reward develops character in kids.

Myth #5—Parents must help kids accomplish as much as possible if they are to develop character.

Myth #6—Parents must emphasize consistently high expectations for their kids. Children must keep reaching in order to be the best they can be.

Myth #7—In today's world, parents have to watch their children carefully and punish them consistently. Our society no longer punishes kids the way it used to. This absence of punishment is hurting them.

Myth #8—Parents must think through rules for their child very carefully because it is these rules that represent the primary control of the child's behavior.

Myth #9—Competition is a bad thing. It is teaching our children some very negative and destructive lessons.

Myth #10—Parents must structure tasks so that kids win. Failure is destructive to a child's ego.

Michael Koehler's commitment to character education grows from a lifetime devoted to education and sports. A grandson of athletic icon Jim Thorpe, Koehler played football at the University of Nebraska, where coaching greats George Kelly and Tom Osborne helped shape his character.

A career educator, Koehler holds a Ph.D. and has worked as a counselor, high school English teacher,  college professor, and administrator. And throughout his academic career, Koehler has coached high school football, helping shape the character of thousands of young athletes for over thirty years.

Koehler lectures widely and has written for the print, radio, and television media. He's also written audio and videotape presentations, as well as numerous education and sports articles. *Coaching Character* is Koehler's sixteenth book.

Koehler now devotes his attention to character education and writing full-time. He and his wife of thirty-nine years spend summers in Minoqua, Wisconsin and winters in Scottsdale, Arizona.